T0305112

FINANCIAL CRISES, LIQUIDITY, AND THE INTERNATIONAL MONETARY SYSTEM

This book is based on the Paolo Baffi Lecture given by the author at the Bank of Italy in October 2000. The Paolo Baffi Lecture is sponsored by the Bank of Italy.

FINANCIAL CRISES, LIQUIDITY, AND THE INTERNATIONAL MONETARY SYSTEM

Jean Tirole

PRINCETON UNIVERSITY PRESS   PRINCETON AND OXFORD

Library of Congress Cataloging-in-Publication Data applied for.
Tirole, Jean
Financial Crises, Liquidity and the International Monetary System /
Jean Tirole
p. cm.
Includes bibliographical references and index.
ISBN 0-691-09985-5 (alk. paper)

British Library Cataloguing-in-Publication Data
A catalogue record for this book is available from the British Library.

This book has been composed in Sabon

www.pup.princeton.edu

10 9 8 7 6 5 4 3 2

Contents _____

Acknowledgments _____

Giving the sixth Paolo Baffi Lecture on Money and Finance is a great privilege and honor for me. When Albert Ando, on behalf of the scientific committee, Governor Fazio and the Bank of Italy, asked me to give the lecture, I was both thrilled and intimidated by the challenge. The distinguished lists of economists who preceded me and the Bank's long-standing tradition of excellence in economic research (a tradition that Governor Baffi helped setting up and that is certainly alive today) provided both high-powered incentives and anxiety.

I could not have written this lecture without the key input of Bengt Holmström (who co-authored with me a series of papers on aggregate liquidity) and Olivier Blanchard. My discussant, Richard Portes, Ricardo Caballero, Paola Caselli, Mathias Dewatripont, Philippe Martin, Larry Summers, Daniele Terlizzese, and especially Curzio Giannini and Olivier Jeanne gave very detailed and useful reactions to a first draft in the fall of 2000. I also thank three reviewers for helpful comments.

Finally, I would like to thank the Bank of Italy for its remarkable hospitality and for making the preparation of this manuscript a real pleasure.

Introduction

A wide consensus had emerged among economists. Capital account liberalization – allowing capital to flow freely in and out of countries without restrictions – was unambiguously good. Good for the debtor countries, good for the world economy. The two-fold case for capital mobility is relatively straightforward: First, capital mobility creates superior insurance opportunities and promotes an efficient allocation of investment and consumption. Capital mobility allows households and firms to insure against country-specific shocks in worldwide markets; households can thereby smooth their consumption and firms better manage their risks. Business cycles are dampened, improved liquidity management boosts investment and promotes growth. Second, besides insurance, capital mobility also permits the transfer of savings from low- to high-return countries. This transfer raises worldwide growth and further gives a chance to the labor force of low-income countries to live better. In these two respects, the increase in the flow of private capital from industrial to developing countries from $174 billion in the 1980s to $1.3 trillion during the 1990s[1] should be considered good news.

That consensus has been shattered lately. A number of capital account liberalizations have been followed by

---

[1] Summers (2000).

spectacular foreign exchange and banking crises.[2] The
past twenty years have witnessed large scale crises such
as those in Latin America (early 1980s), Scandinavia
(early 1990s), Mexico (1994), Thailand, Indonesia, and
South Korea (1997), Russia (1998), Brazil (1998–9) and
Argentina (2001), as well as many smaller episodes. The
crises have imposed substantial welfare losses on
hundreds of millions of people in those countries.

Economists, as we will discuss later, still strongly
favor some form of capital mobility but are currently
widely divided about the interpretation of the crises
and especially their implications for capital controls
and the governance of the international financial system.
Are such crises just an undesirable, but unavoidable by-
product of an otherwise desirable full capital account
liberalization? Should the world evolve either to the
corporate model where workouts are a regular non-crisis
event or to the municipal bond model where defaults are
rare? Would a better sequencing (e.g., liberalization of
foreign direct and portfolio investments and the building
of stronger institutions for the prudential supervision of
financial intermediaries before the liberalization of
short-term capital flows) have prevented these episodes?
Should temporary or permanent restrictions on short-
term capital flows be imposed? How does this all fit
with the choice of an exchange rate regime? Were the
crises handled properly? And, should our international
financial institutions be reformed?

This book was prompted by a questioning of my own
understanding of its subject. Several times over recent
years I have been swayed by a well-expounded and
coherent proposal only to discover, with striking naivety,

[2] 131 of the 181 IMF member countries have experienced banking
problems between 1980 and 1995 (IMF 1996).

that I later found an equally eloquent, but inconsistent, argument just as persuasive. While this probably reflected lazy thinking on my part, I also came to wonder how it is that economists whom I respect very highly could agree broadly on the facts and yet disagree strongly on their implications.

I also realized that I was missing a "broad picture". An epitome for this lack of perspective relates to international institutions. I have never had a clear view of what, leaving aside the fight against poverty, the International Monetary Fund (IMF) and other international financial institutions (IFIs) were trying to achieve: avoid financial crises, resolve them in an orderly manner, economize on taxpayers' money, protect foreign investors, respect national sovereignty, limit output volatility, prevent contagion, facilitate a country's access to funds, promote long-term growth, force structural reforms – not to mention the IMF's traditional current account, international reserves and inflation objectives.[3]

This book is to some extent an attempt to go back to first principles and to identify a specific form of market failure, that will guide our thinking about crisis prevention and institutional design. Needless to say, I will be focusing on a particular take on the international financial system, which need not exclude other and complementary approaches. I believe, though, that the specific angle taken here may prove useful in clarifying the issues.

The book is organized as follows. Chapter 1 is a concise overview of recent crises and institutional moves for the reader with limited familiarity with the

[3] For example, the Meltzer Commission, or more precisely the International Financial Institution Advisory Commission, chaired by Alan Meltzer and reporting to the US Congress (2000), views the role of the IMF as limiting the incidence of crises, reducing their severity, duration and spillovers.

topic. Chapter 2 summarizes and offers a critique of economists' views on the subject. Chapter 3 provides a roadmap for our main argument. Basically, I suggest that international financing is similar to standard corporate financing except in two crucial respects, which I name the "dual-agency problem" and the "common-agency problem". Chapter 4 therefore provides the reader with a concise review of those key insights of corporate finance that are relevant for international finance. Chapter 5 describes the market failure. Chapter 6 draws its implications for crisis prevention and management. Chapter 7 investigates the lessons of the analysis for the design of international financial institutions.Finally, Chapter 8 summarizes and discusses routes for future research.

FINANCIAL CRISES, LIQUIDITY, AND THE INTERNATIONAL MONETARY SYSTEM

1

Emerging Markets Crises and Policy Responses

Many excellent books and articles have documented the new breed of "twenty-first century" financial crises.[1] I will therefore content myself with a *short overview* of the main developments. This chapter can be skipped by readers who are familiar with Emerging Markets (EM) crises.

The pre-crisis period

No two crises are identical. At best we can identify a set of features common to most if not all episodes. Let us begin with a list of frequent sources of vulnerability in recent capital-account crises.

Size and nature of capital inflows. The new breed of crises was preceded by financial liberalization and very large capital inflows. In particular the removal of controls on capital outflows (the predominant form of capital control) has led to massive and rapid inflows of capital.

---

[1] E.g., Bordo et al (2001), Caballero (2000), Corsetti (1999), De Gregorio et al (1999), Dornbusch (1998), Eichengreen (1999a), Fischer (1998a,b), Hunter et al (1999), Kenen (2000), McKinnon–Pill (1990), Mussa et al (1999), Obsfeld–Rogoff (1998), Portes (1999), Rogoff (1999), Sachs–Radelet (1995), Sachs–Warner (1995), Summers (1999, 2000), Woo et al (2000), World Bank (1997, 1998), World Economic Outlook (1998). Some observers establish a finer distinction between the crises of the 1980s and those of the 1990s. Michel Camdessus, former IMF managing director, called the 1994–5 Mexican crisis the first financial crisis of the 21st century. There is little purpose in engaging in such a distinction given the limited purpose of this chapter.

Instead of inducing onshore capital to flow offshore to earn higher returns, these removals have enhanced the appeal of borrowing countries to foreign investors by signaling the governments' willingness to keep the doors unlocked.[2]

At the aggregate level, the net capital flows to developing countries exceeded $240 bn in 1996 ($265 bn if South Korea is included), six times the number at the beginning of the decade, and four times the peak reached during the 1978–82 commercial lending boom.[3] Capital inflows represented a substantial fraction of gross domestic product (GDP) in a number of countries: 9.4 percent for Brazil (1992–5), 25.8 percent for Chile (1989–95), 9.3 percent in Korea (1991–5), 45.8 percent in Malaysia (1989–95), 27.1 percent in Mexico (1989–94) and 51.5 percent in Thailand (1988–95).[4]

This growth in foreign investment has been accompanied by a shift in its nature, a shift in lender composition, and a shift in recipients. Before the 1980s, medium-term loans issued by syndicates of commercial banks to sovereign states and public sector entities accounted for a large share of private capital flows to developing countries, and official flows to these countries were commensurate with private flows.

Today private capital flows dwarf official flows. On the recipient side,[5] borrowing by the public sector has shrunk

---

[2] For such a signal to be credible, though, a government that is committed to capital-account liberalization must find it less costly to lift controls on capital outflows than a government that is not committed. See Bartolini–Drazen (1997) for a formalization of this idea.

[3] World Bank (1997).

[4] World Bank (1997).

[5] See Gourinchas et al (1999) for evidence on lending booms. Among other things, this paper suggests that lending booms are not damaging to the economy, although they substantially increase the probability of a banking or balance of payment crisis. Also, the proportion of short-term debt rises with investment during the build-up phase.

to less than one-fifth of total private flows.[6] As for the composition of private flows, the share of foreign direct investment (FDI) has grown from 15 percent in 1990 to 40 percent, and that of global portfolio bond and equity flows grew from a negligible level at the beginning of the decade to about 33 percent in 1997. Bank lending has evolved toward short-term, foreign currency denominated debt. Such foreign bank debt, mostly denominated in dollars and with maturity under a year, reached 45 percent of GDP in Thailand, 35 percent in Indonesia and 25 percent in Korea just before the Asian crisis.[7]

There are several reasons for the sharp increase in the capital flows in the last twenty years:[8] the ideological shift to free markets and the privatizations in developing countries; the arrival of supporting infrastructure such as telecommunications and international standards on banking supervision and accounting; the regulatory changes that made it possible for the pension funds,

---

[6] World Bank (1997).

[7] The Economist (1999).

[8] See De Gregorio et al (1999) and The Economist (1999) for a lengthier discussion of the sharp increase in capital flows from developed countries to developing countries. We should note, though, that despite this sharp increase it is still the case that a small amount of capital flows from rich to poor countries. Kraay et al (2000) present useful evidence on "country portfolios". Based on a sample of 68 countries, accounting for over 90 percent of world production, from 1966 through 1997, they show among other things that countries hold small gross asset positions and that these assets are mainly loans. For example, industrial countries hold about 3.3 percent and 3.9 percent of their wealth in foreign equity assets and liabilities. These proportions are about 11 percent for foreign loan assets and liabilities. Relatedly, it is well known that individuals hardly hedge risks across countries. Over 90 percent of US and Japanese financial portfolios (and 89 percent and 85 percent of French and German portfolios) are invested in domestic assets (French–Poterba 1991), which furthermore are positively correlated with the individuals' non-financial wealth (human capital). It is also well-known that consumption is less correlated across countries than output, in contrast to what portfolio diversification would suggest. See Lewis (1999) for a thorough survey of the home bias in equities and consumption.

banks, mutual funds, and insurance companies of developed countries to invest abroad; the perception of new, high-yield investment opportunities in Emerging-Market economies; and the new expertise associated with the development of the Brady bond market.[9]

Banking fragility. Up to the 1970s, balance of payment crises were largely unrelated to bank failures. The banking industry was highly regulated, and banking activity was much more limited and far less risky than it is now. It operated mostly at the national level and foreign borrowings were strictly constrained by exchange controls. Various regulations, such as licensing restrictions and interest rate ceilings, kept banks from competing against each other. There were also far fewer financial markets and derivative instruments to play with.

The 1970s and 1980s witnessed a trend toward openness and deregulation, but the subsequent expansion in banking activities and exposure in capital markets made banking riskier. In response, the Basle Committee on Banking Supervision in the past several years has been involved in instituting new banking regulations, concerning minimum capital standards for credit risk (the Basle Accord in 1988), and risk management (the 1996 Amendment to the Accord to account for market risk on the banks' trading book), and is proposing some further reforms.

A common feature of the new breed of crises is the fragility of the banking system prior to the crisis.[10]

---

[9] Calvo (1998, 2000) argues that the securitization of non-performing sovereign debt under the Brady plan forced financial institutions to learn about the economies' fundamentals and made them more willing to buy securities in the corresponding countries.

[10] This fact is well documented by Kaminsky and Reinhart (1999). See also Goldfajn–Valdes (1997) for an analysis of Chile, Finland, Mexico and Sweden.

Often, the relaxation of controls on foreign borrowing took place without adequate supervision. For example, banking problems played a central role in the Latin American crises of the early 1980s.[11] The widespread insolvency of Chilean institutions in 1981–4 resulted in the Chilean government guaranteeing all foreign debts of the Chilean banking system and owning 70 percent of the banking system in 1985. Similarly, the banks of the East Asian countries that suffered crises in 1997 (Thailand, Korea, Indonesia, Malaysia) were very poorly capitalized. [More generally, overleverage was not confined to banks as firms' balance sheets also deteriorated prior to the crises. For example, leverage doubled in Malaysia and Thailand between 1991 and 1996, according to the World Bank (1997).]

Currency and maturity mismatch. Some of the domestic debt and virtually all of the external debt of EM economies is denominated in foreign currency, with very little hedging of exchange rate risk, a phenomenon labeled "liability dollarization" by Calvo (1998). For example, before the Asian Crisis, Thailand, Korea, and Indonesia created incentives to borrow abroad through implicit and explicit guarantees and other policy-induced incentives.[12] To be certain, banking regulations usually mandate currency matching, but such regulations have often been weakly enforced. Furthermore, even if the banks' books are formally matched, they may be subject to a substantial foreign exchange risk through their non-bank borrowers' risk of default. For

---

[11] See, e.g., Diaz–Alejandro (1985) and Harberger (1985).

[12] For example, Thailand offered tax breaks on offshore foreign borrowing. In contrast, Taiwan had well-capitalized banks with little currency and maturity mismatches. Despite a contagious attack on its currency, which forced officials to float the rate, the Taiwanese economy suffered little from the 1997 crisis.

example, the Indonesian private sector engaged heavily in liability dollarization, and so the banks faced an important "credit risk" (de facto a foreign exchange risk) with those borrowers who had borrowed in foreign currencies.

The second type of mismatch was on the maturity side. For instance, 60 percent of the $380 bn of international bank debt outstanding in Asia at the end of 1997 had maturity of less than one year.[13] Often, the short-term bias has been viewed favorably and even encouraged by policymakers. Mexico increased its resort to de facto short-term (dollar-denominated) government debt, the Tesobonos, before the 1995 crisis. South Korea favored short-term borrowings and discriminated against long-term capital inflows. Thailand mortgaged all of its government reserves on forward markets. As documented by Detragiache–Spilimbergo (2001), short debt maturities increase the probability of debt crises, although the causality may, as they argue, flow in the reverse direction (more fragile countries may be forced to borrow at shorter maturities).

Macroeconomic evolution. Despite attempts at sterilizing capital inflows[14] in many countries, aggregate demand and asset prices grew. Real estate prices went up substantially.

In contrast with earlier crises, which had usually been preceded by large fiscal deficits, the new ones offered

---

[13] The Economist (1999).

[14] Remember that a non-sterilized intervention is similar to an open market operation except that the assets purchased are foreign assets rather than domestic ones; it therefore impacts the domestic monetary base. To avoid affecting the domestic monetary base, the Central Bank can engage in an offsetting domestic intervention by selling domestic bonds. Thus, in reduced form, a sterilized intervention amounts to purchasing foreign assets by selling domestic ones (or the reverse).

more variation in fiscal matters. While some countries (such as Brazil and Russia) did incur large fiscal deficits, many others, including the Asian countries, had no or small fiscal deficits.

Poor institutional infrastructure. Many crisis countries have been marred by poor governance, low investor protection, connected lending, inefficient bankruptcy laws and enforcement, lack of transparency, and poor application of accounting standards.

Currency regime. As Stan Fischer (testifying to the Meltzer Commission, 2000) notes, all countries that have lately suffered major international crises had fixed exchange rates (or crawling pegs in the case of Indonesia and Korea).

Summers (2000) usefully summarizes the major sources of vulnerability in recent major capital-account crises. As Table 1 shows, traditional determinants of exchange-rate crises (current-account and fiscal deficits) played a role in only some economies. In contrast, banking weaknesses and a short debt maturity seem to have been present in most of the crises.

The crisis

Crises are usually characterized by the following features (in no particular chronological order):

Sudden reversals in net private capital flows. Large reversals of capital flows in a short time interval had a substantial impact on the economies. The reversal reached 12 percent and 6 percent of GDP in Mexico in 1981–3 and 1993–5, respectively, 20 percent in Argentina in 1982–3, and 7 percent in Chile in 1981–3.[15] In

---

[15] World Bank (1997, Figure 1.5).

Table 1
Sources of vulnerabilities in recent major capital-account[a]

Source	Country					
	Brazil	Indonesia	South Korea	Mexico	Thailand	Russia
Pegged exchange rate (reserve depletion)	1	0.5[b]	0.5	1	1	1
Current-account deficit	0.5	2	3	1	1	3
Fiscal deficit	1	3	3	3	3	1
Banking and financial sector weakness	3	1	1	1	1	1
Government short-term debt	1	3	3	1	2	1
Total short-term foreign indebtedness	2	1	1	2	1	1
General governance	2	1	2	2	2	1

[a] *Notes:* Key to table entries: 1, very serious; 2, serious; 3, not central.
[b] Indonesia let its exchange rate float in August 1998, did exhibit strong signs of real exchange-rate misalignment, and did not expend reserves defending the rate. However, the inflexible exchange-rate regime does seem to have encouraged a large buildup of foreign currency debt in the private sector. (Source: Summers 2000).

Indonesia, Korea, Malaysia, Philippines, and Thailand, the combined difference between the 1997 outflows and 1996 inflows equaled $85 bn, or about 10 percent of these countries' GDPs.

Exchange rate depreciation/devaluation. Most countries suffering a crisis were countries with well-integrated capital accounts and with a fixed exchange rate (or crawling peg). The attacks forced the central banks to abandon the peg or more generally to let their currency depreciate. Figure 1 illustrates this in the case of Asian crises. For example, South Korea's won lost half of its value in 1997. Thailand devalued by 15 percent and after the IMF got involved the baht lost a further 50 percent. The Mexican peso lost 50 percent of its value in a week in December 1994 before the IMF intervened. The exchange rate depreciation reduced incomes and spending.

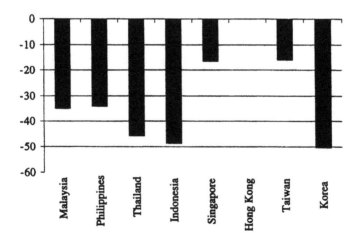

Figure 1.   Asian exchange rate changes, 1997. US dollar per currency, percentage change, 1 January–31 December. (Source Christoffersen–Errunga 2000)

Activity and asset prices. Bank restructuring proved very costly.[16] Fiscal costs associated with bank restructurings averaged 10 percent of GDP and have reached much higher values. Furthermore, whether banks were liquidated or just put on a tighter leash (which was the case for 40 percent of asset holdings in the case of Korean, Malaysian, and Thai banks), restructuring resulted in a credit crunch, which, combined with the firms' own difficulties, led to severe recessions, in particular in the non-tradable goods sector. Indeed, in Indonesia, Korea, and Thailand, many banks in 1998 not only stopped issuing new loans, but also cut back on trade credit and working capital.

Equity (see, e.g., Figure 2 for Asian countries) and real estate prices tumbled. As stressed by Krugman (1998), the fall in prices resulted in a wave of inward direct investment just after massive flights of short-term capital out of those countries. For example, FDI at fire sale prices occurred in South Korea, whose currency had lost half of its value relative to the dollar, and whose stock market had lost 40 percent of its value in domestic currency. This wave of fire sale FDI in some instances (e.g., in Malaysia) gave rise to political concerns of colonization or recolonization.

Contagion. Some recent crises raised serious concerns about contagion. Contagion occurred in Europe in the

---

[16] Estimates provided by Rojas-Suarez–Weisbrod (1996) put the bill for bank restructuring at 19.6 percent of GDP for Chile and 13 percent for Argentina in the early 1980s, and from 4.5 percent to 8.2 percent of GDP for the Scandinavian countries in the late 1980s-early 1990s. Caprio–Monahan (1999) estimate an average cost of government bailouts in a sample of 59 banking crashes to be 9 percent of GDP in developing countries and 4 percent of GDP in industrialized countries. See also Frydl (1999)'s survey.

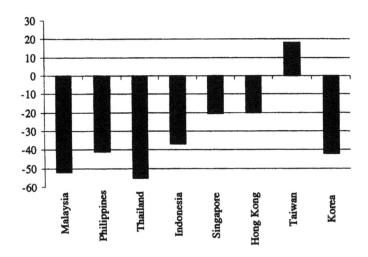

Figure 2. Asian stock price changes, 1997. Local currency, percentage change, 1 January–31 December. (Source Christoffersen–Errunga 2000)

ERM crises of 1992–3, in Latin America following the 1994–5 Mexican problems (the Tequila crisis), and in Asia in 1997–8 starting with the crisis in Thailand (the Asian flu). While spillovers have been mostly regional, there are also indications that they can be more widespread. For example, the August 1998 Russian crisis spread to Brazil in the fall, triggering the January 1999 crisis, and started spreading to other Latin American emerging markets. Even though the fundamentals in Brazil were weak (large public deficits and uncertainty about the government's ability to roll over the public debt), this episode dramatically illustrates the global nature of spillovers.

There are several competing hypotheses for the contagious aspect of crises. The *portfolio rebalancing* hypothesis states that after losing money in one country foreign investors have to readjust their positions in other countries. For example, when Russian markets collapsed, some large portfolio managers faced margin calls and liquidated their positions in Brazil. Kaminsky et al (2000) argue and offer evidence that mutual fund managers prefer to sell in markets that are mostly liquid, as they incur smaller losses in such markets. Capital adequacy requirements may force banks to adopt similar strategies. Van Rijckeghem and Weder (2000), noting that western and Japanese banks had substantial exposures in the four Asian crisis countries (Korea, Indonesia, Malaysia, Thailand), present evidence for the hypothesis that a crisis in a country may spread to countries with common foreign bank lenders, as in the case of Thailand and maybe Mexico and Russia. It is unclear, though, why investors would deprive themselves of very lucrative arbitrage opportunities by failing to manage their regional risks.

A second hypothesis is the *trade links hypothesis*, which has two versions. In the first, a crisis in a country has repercussions on countries that are tightly commercially related. For example, the collapse of the Soviet Union had a non-negligible impact on Finland. In the second, competitive devaluation version, crises lead to substantial devaluations and increased competition for countries producing similar exports.

The third hypothesis relates to the *existence of common shocks* (rise in interest rates, increase in the price of oil, perceived change in the international community's willingness to come to the rescue). Although there is then no systemic effect so to speak, the crises exhibit a strong correlation. The fourth, and final, hypothesis is a *change in expectations*. The wake-up-call story asserts that investors realize the lack of solidity of certain types of economies or the unwillingness of the IMF to help restructure the debt.[17] Each of these hypotheses probably has some validity, and current research is actively disentangling their respective impacts in specific crises.[18]

Rescue packages. The international community, often through the IMF,[19] designed rescue packages of an

[17] Still another hypothesis is that contagion is triggered by the correlation of "sunspots" across countries in situations of multiple equilibria (Masson 1999a,b). For example, foreign investors in country B view the fact that there is a run on country A as a signal that there will be a run in country B and engage in a self-fulfilling run.

[18] See, e.g., Chang–Majnoni (2000), Corsetti et al (2000), De Gregorio–Valdes (2000), Dornbusch et al (2000), Goldfajn–Baig (2000), Kaminsky et al (2000) and Van Rijckeghem–Weder (2000).

[19] The IMF's role as a crisis manager has expanded over the last few years. Although present, the Fund's crisis management mission was certainly not emphasized in the 1944 Articles of Agreement: "The purposes of the International Monetary Fund are:

(i)   To promote international monetary cooperation through a permanent institution which provides the machinery for consultation and collaboration on international monetary problems.

(ii) To facilitate the expansion and balanced growth of international trade, and to contribute thereby to the promotion and maintenance of high levels of employment and real income and to the development of the productive resources of all members as primary objectives of economic policy.

(iii) To promote exchange stability, to maintain orderly exchange arrangements among members, and to avoid competitive exchange depreciation.

(iv) To assist in the establishment of a multilateral system of payments in respect of current transactions between members and in the elimination of foreign exchange restrictions which hamper the growth of world trade.

(v)   To give confidence to members by making the general resources of the Fund temporarily available to them under adequate safeguards, thus providing them with opportunity to correct maladjustments in their balance of payments without resorting to measures destructive of national or international prosperity.

(vi) In accordance with the above, to shorten the duration and lessen the degree of disequilibrium in the international balances of payments of members. The Fund shall be guided in all its policies and decisions by the purposes set forth in this Article." (Article I).

unprecedented scale (see Table 2). The 1995 Mexican rescue package involved $50 bn or 18 times the country's quota (while IMF loans have traditionally been limited to three times a country's quota),[20] and similar size packages were offered in Asia in 1997: $57 bn in Korea, $40 bn in Indonesia, and $17.2 bn in Thailand. It should be borne in mind, though, that despite their huge size, such packages by themselves were unlikely to restrain speculative attacks on the currencies. For example, IMF packages in Thailand, South Korea, and Indonesia were much smaller than the countries' short-term foreign liabilities. Besides, even IMF packages that would have been as large as the countries' short-term liabilities might not have been sufficient to prevent the crises; Jeanne and Wyplosz (2001) present some evidence that capital outflows were typically larger than the decrease in short-term liabilities during the crises.[21]

Investor bail-in. The degree of sharing by foreign investors has been crisis-specific. Under the Brady plan (debt writedowns for Latin American countries), creditors got one-third of the face value of their outstanding claim. Investors cashed out at full value in Mexico in 1995. They lost up to $350 bn in total in Asia in 1997 and Russia in 1998.[22]

Global solutions have favored bondholders relative to equity investors (foreign direct investment and equity portfolio investment). Forcing private investors to share the burden has proved hard in the case of sovereign

[20] Total rescue packages can exceed the IMF's treble-quota limit as a) they may involve bilateral creditors or other IFIs, and b) the IMF limit may be exceeded in case of contagious (systemic) impact.

[21] See also Bernard–Bisignano (2000). Relatedly, Haldane (1999), reviewing the evidence, concludes that IMF rescue packages fail to reassure investors.

[22] This number is given by Hildebrand in De Gregorio et al (1999, p118).

Table 2 IMF-supported crisis packages of the 1990s: Total financing and outstanding obligations to IMF (in percent of initial GDP [a]) (Source: Jeanne-Zettelmeyer 2000)

	Date of program approval	Financing Commitments		Disbursements under program		Credits outstanding on IMF program [b,c]	Total 1999 IMF credits outstanding [c]
		Total	IMF	Total	IMF		
Mexico	Feb-95	18.3	6.3	9.1	4.6	0.9	1.4
Thailand	Aug-97	11.5	2.7	9.6	2.3	2.1	2.1
Indonesia	Nov-97	19.6	5.2	9.3	4.8	4.3	4.3
Korea	Dec-97	12.3	4.4	6.5	4.1	1.2	1.2
Brazil	Dec-98	5.4	2.3	3.3	1.4	1.1	1.1
Memorandum Item [d]							
Russia					6.6[e]	n.a	4.1

[a] GDP in first year of large package (1997 for Indonesia, Korea and Thailand, 1995 for Mexico and Russia, and 1998 for Brazil)
[b] IMF disbursements minus repurchases by end-99 *related to the program.*
[c] Discounted to the first program year using IMF rate of charge
[d] Russia had several consecutive IMF programs during the 1990s. The first large-scale program was a stand-by arrangement approved in April of 1995.
[e] Total Disbursements in the 1990s

bonds. For example, Eichengreen and Rühl (2000), in studying the extent of bail-ins in Ecuador, Pakistan, Romania, and Ukraine, conclude that attempts at forcing private investors to share the burden have had limited success overall, but have been a little more successful where renegotiation-facilitating collective action clauses were appended to the bonds (Pakistan and Ukraine).

A typical debt restructuring proceeds in the following manner: some fiscal and other adjustment is demanded from the country while bilateral official creditors (the Paris Club) agree to rollover or reschedule some debt claims, and multilateral creditors (the IMF, the World Bank (WB), and other multilateral development banks) bring in new money. The rest of the external financing gap is meant to be covered by the private creditors through "private sector involvement" (PSI). The level of multilateral support is relatively well determined. IMF and WB lending receives priority. The claims of bilateral creditors are junior, and last come private claims. Roubini (2000) argues, though, that Paris Club claims are definitely not senior to private creditors' claims: unlike the latter, they are not subject to litigation risk or acceleration[23] or formal default. Accordingly, some countries have kept access to financial markets even though they were in arrears with bilateral official creditors.[24]

Conditionality. Besides the general prohibition of actions such as the introduction of new exchange restric-

---

[23] "Acceleration" refers to the possibility for a category of debtholders to demand early reimbursement if there is default on another claim.

[24] See Roubini (2000) for a broad discussion of PSI, including the issue of which claims ought to be included (should PSI include bonded debt, short-term interbank loans, Euro bonds, domestic debts?) and that of whether PSI should be accompanied by exchange rate and capital controls.

tions specified in the Articles of Agreement, the IMF usually imposes further, country-specific conditions. Traditionally, the IMF performs an in-depth analysis of the sources of economic imbalances. Until the 1970s and the 1980s, its conditions focused on current account balance and its macroeconomic determinants (most notably monetary and fiscal policies). Under sharp criticism concerning its narrow focus, the IMF then added medium-term growth.

More recently, and in particular with the Asian crises, the IMF, while pursuing the traditional current account determinants,[25] has added *microeconomic* programs such as[26]

- the closure of insolvent financial institutions (Korea, Indonesia, Thailand), and the recapitalization of others with explicitly limited public funds (all countries)
- the strengthening of prudential regulation (all countries)
- the liberalization of foreign investments in domestic banks (Korea, Indonesia, Thailand)
- the closure of non-viable firms (Korea) and the restructuring of corporate debts (Indonesia, Korea, Thailand)
- the strengthening of the legal infrastructure and enforcement (competition policy, bankruptcy laws, corporate governance, privatization, etc.)
- the reduction of import tariffs and export taxes (Indonesia), and
- the design of social policies to protect low-income groups and the unemployed, and health and education programs.

---

[25] In this respect, demands such as improvements in tax collection (Russia) and the reduction in local spending (Brazil) are traditional ones.

[26] See World Economic Outlook (1998, p105) for a broader list.

Even observers favorable to conditionality, such as Goldstein (2001), have wondered whether the IMF was not suffering from a "mission creep". And a number of economists, including Feldstein (1998a,b), have advocated a return to the old mandate of pursuing macroeconomic and currency stabilization.

A different type of criticism leveled at IMF conditionality relates to the programs' credibility. IMF policy conditions are often renegotiated, sometimes (as in Asia) within a few weeks of the programs being agreed. For example, Indonesia, Korea, and Thailand were quickly allowed to incur a small budget deficit, and capital adequacy and bank closure requirements were relaxed for Indonesia and Thailand.[27]

IMF reforms, regulatory changes, and private sector innovations

Besides the new emphasis on microconditionality, IMF policy has undergone a number of changes:
- *Code of good practices*: The IMF has issued a code of good practices for fiscal and monetary policies.
- *Information collection and surveillance*: The IMF has launched a Special Data Dissemination Standard (SDDS), which provides a checklist of the country's financial and economic data. In collaboration with the WB, and in consultation with supervisory agencies, central banks, and the private sector, the IMF collects and analyzes information published in the reports on the Observance of Standards and Codes.

[27] See Radelet–Sachs (1998) for more detail. Further thoughts about IMF programs can be found in Dixit (2000), Kaufman–Kruger (2000), Hunter (1999), Masson (1999), Mussa–Savastano (1999)

- *New forms of lending*: The Supplemental Reserve
Facility (SRF), created by the IMF in December
1997 and first used in Korea, allows the IMF to
make large short-term[28] loans at rates higher than it
normally charges. SFRs have quickly developed into a
major form of IMF lending. In April 1999, the IMF
established a no-penalty-rate Contingent Credit Line
(CCL) to facilitate a rapid disbursement to pre-quali-
fied members. The drawing of the line is contingent on
the IMF's judgement about whether the country has
contributed to its problems. The country must apply
in advance for a CCL.[29]

Besides IMF reforms, experiments are underway that
aim at providing private solutions to country-level
problems. While the credit lines involved are relatively
small and therefore very unlikely per se to prevent a
crisis, these experiments are worth considering. The
pioneer in the area was Argentina (Mexico, Indonesia,
and South Africa have reached similar agreements).
Argentina had been badly hurt by the Mexican Tequila
crisis, with a drop in deposits of the order of 18 percent
during a three-month period and a 5 percent drop in
GDP. On December 20, 1996, the Central Bank agreed
with fourteen international banks on a firm commitment
$6.1bn (8 percent of the deposit base) liquidity option.

[28] For longer-term (say, over three years) adjustments of macroeconomic
imbalances, the IMF can use different programs: the Extended Fund Facility
(EFF), and the Enhanced Structural Adjustment Facility (ESAF, at low interest
rates for low-income countries).

[29] The Meltzer Commission report of February 2000 argues that, together
with the existence of other channels for IMF money, the application requirement explains why no country had yet applied at the date of the report. The
commission's argument is that an application would be interpreted as a signal
of an impending crisis. In September 2000, the IMF tried to enhance the
appeal of the Contingent Credit Line by getting rid of the commitment fee,
by reducing the interest rate penalty, and by relaxing conditions for prequalification.

According to the agreement, the Central Bank had the option to sell domestic assets,[30] such as government bonds, to receive US dollars subject to a repurchase clause. The average maturity of the program was three years; the average commitment fee, 32.5 basis points; and the interest rate, roughly 2 percent above LIBOR. The credit line was mostly unconditional, as the Central Bank could exercise the options as long as the country had not defaulted on its international debt.[31]

The credit line was meant to be a last line of defense to prevent a run on the banking system. Banks were subject to a remunerated liquidity requirement in international reserves equal to 20 percent of deposits. Adding the Central Bank's excess international reserves (10 percent of the deposit base), the credit line with private financial institutions was at the time of the agreement meant to step in only in case of a liquidity shock exceeding 30 percent of the deposit base.

As Giannini (2000) points out, however, we should not expect such arrangements to be a perfect substitute for public money. First, and as we have already noted, the amounts involved are relatively limited. Second, they must remain proper credit lines. If such credit lines are secured with high-quality collateral and, further, are subject to margin calls, they do little to enhance a country's liquidity. That is, the credit line substitutes for the collateral as a source of liquidity; and margin calls eliminate some of the insurance that

---

[30] There was overcollateralization: Argentinian bonds had to exceed by 25 percent the value of funds delivered. WB/IDB resources are used to cover further margin calls, making the contingent liquidity facility not a purely private arrangement.

[31] The Mexican government has arranged an overdraft facility for about $3 bn. Amusingly, the government's decision to draw $2.66 bn in September 1998 aroused much controversy among lending banks (the market interest rates had gone up since the writing of the arrangement).

is the essence of a credit line. Third, and importantly, the banks involved in the arrangement may wish to hedge their exposure, for example by selling government securities short. Such behavior may undo country risk management, as country borrowing is the sum of private and government borrowings from foreigners.

Finally, prudential supervisors are changing the rules that regulate the financial institutions' investments in Emerging Market countries. Designing good prudential rules is in general quite difficult, and particularly so in the case of cross-border investments. For example, the 1988 Basle Accord, which harmonizes capital adequacy requirements for banks, requires an equity level of 8 cents per dollar (a risk weight of 100 percent) invested in a loan (with maturity over a year) to a non-OECD bank or sovereign, 0 cents for an investment in an OECD sovereign bond, and 1.6 cents (risk weight of 20 percent) for a loan to an OECD bank. Clearly, the binary criterion "OECD-non OECD" poorly accounts for individual situations. Ironically, Mexico and Korea became OECD members just before their respective crises, which further fueled bank loans to those countries.[32]

The creation of new derivative instruments and the banks' ability to take indirect exposures through interactions with hedge funds that are highly exposed to interest rate and exchange rate fluctuations (such as Long Term Capital Management during the 1998 Russian crisis) raises new challenges for prudential regulation. For example, while there is no reason to regulate hedge funds, which in particular are not backed by public money, the banks' portfolio, credit, and counterparty

[32] According to the Bank for International Settlements, bank loans to developing countries totaled $931 bn, of which $520 bn was in short-term loans in December 1997.

risks incurred in the interaction with such funds must be properly assessed by prudential regulators.

The new rules proposed in June 1999 by the Basel Committee on Banking Supervision include the use of ratings of sovereign debt in the determination of risk weights, and would leave open the possibility for large banks of using their internal ratings (following the so-called 'internal model approach'). Such ratings would of course accelerate flights of capital out of countries that are starting to experience distress. They would induce banks to scramble for exits (and probably to lend short), on the basis that advanced countries' bank owners are playing with public money and not just their own.[33]

---

[33] Monfort–Mulder (2000) estimate that the banks' capital requirements corresponding to their exposure on Emerging Market lending would have increased by 40 percent under the proposed modification to the Basle Accord. They also question the relevance of the sovereign ratings provided by rating agencies.

2

The Economists' Views

Many of the best minds among economists and the financial community have expressed their views on recent international financial crises and the design of a new financial infrastructure.[1] While there is widespread agreement on what happened, there is much less convergence on what should be done about it. Still, we can identify a common core of proposals (together with, as usual, a few dissenting voices), as well as a number of issues on which economists disagree. Abusing terminology, let us call the former the "consensus view".

Consensus view

The seven pillars of the consensus view

Most recommendations concur on a number of desirable steps:

• *Elimination of currency mismatches.* A high level of indebtedness in foreign currencies makes a country very vulnerable to a depreciation in the exchange rate and to the concomitant liquidity and solvency risk faced by domestic banks and firms. Along with this, the absence of countrywide risk management confronts monetary

---

[1] The reader will find much useful material on the topic in Nouriel Roubini's remarkable website: http://www.stern.nyu.edu/~nroubini/.

policy with an unpalatable dilemma.[2] A tight monetary policy, to maintain the exchange rate, runs the risk of a severe recession, while a loose monetary policy leads to depreciation of the currency and possibly the bankruptcy of firms and banks that are highly indebted in foreign currency.

A common proposal, therefore, is to eliminate currency mismatches, at least at the level of banks and the government. Furthermore, many suggest that a domestic build-up of international reserves would reassure foreign investors about the value of their investment.

• *Elimination of maturity mismatches.* To prevent hot money from fleeing the country, many advocate a lengthening in debt maturity, as well as measures encouraging alternatives to short-term debt, such as foreign direct investment (FDI) and investment by foreign bank subsidiaries.

• *Better institutional infrastructure.* In response to the poor governance that has marred many crisis countries, the consensus view argues that infrastructure-promoting reforms, such as adherence to universal principles for securities market regulation designed by the International Organization of Securities Commission (IOSCO) and those for accounting designed by the International Accounting Standards Committee (IASC), would reassure foreign investors and help prevent crises.

• *Better prudential supervision.* Most crisis countries' prudential regulations satisfied the international standards as defined by the Basle Accord (1988, revised in 1996). It is in the nature of such standards to be highly imperfect (despite much effort devoted to their design by

---

[2] Aghion et al (1999, 2001), Bacchetta (2000) and Krugman (1999). See Kenen (2001, chapter 3) for a review of the empirical evidence.

the Basle Committee on Banking Supervision) and to leave substantial discretion with the national supervisory authorities. Indeed, enforcement of the standards in a number of crisis countries has been highly negligent, resulting in low capital adequacy and high values at risk. The consensus view calls for a better enforcement of existing prudential regulations.

• *Country-level transparency*. Most economists recommend that foreign investors be informed in a uniform and regular manner of the country's structure of guaranteed debt and off-balance-sheet liabilities.

• *Bail-ins*. There is widespread agreement on the desirability (although not on the feasibility) of forcing the foreign investors to share the burden in a case of crisis.[3] The argument is that bailing-in the investors will force them to act in a more responsible manner in lending only to countries with good fundamentals.

There is disagreement fundamentals about whether bail-ins are indeed feasible for short-term debt claims (in the absence of mandated rollover). While there is a consensus around the view that bail-ins of bondholders may be facilitated by the existence of collective action clauses (in the same way that investors had to share the losses on the syndicated bank loans of the 1970s), De Gregorio et al (1999) argue that the bail-in policy is not time-consistent as international financial institutions (IFIs) are unlikely to stay passive and let the crisis unfold when bondholders refuse to write down some of their claims. Eichengreen and Rühl (2000) concur and add that even if bail-ins are successful in a given country, they may induce investors to readjust their

---

[3] Rubin, then the US Secretary of the Treasury, spoke to that effect on April 21, 1999. See also America's Council on Foreign Relations (1999), Eichengreen (1999), and Sachs–Woo (2000).

portfolios toward large countries, with systemic implications, in which bail-ins are less likely.

• *Avoid fixed exchange rates.* The reader will probably be surprised that, in this discussion of economists' consensus views on international crises, I kept views on exchange rate regimes for later. There are two reasons for this. First, many of the recent crises seem to have been triggered by fundamentals somewhat unrelated to exchange rate regimes. The exchange rate regime, however, has an important impact on crisis resolution and its consequences. Second, there is both a consensus and conflicting advice. The broad consensus [4] is that fixed exchange rates work poorly under financial deregulation and that countries with open capital account should choose between floating rates and hard pegs. [5]

Burnside et al (1999, 2001) suggest abandoning fixed rates as soon as possible, and the Meltzer Commission (2000) and Sachs–Woo (2000) recommend avoiding pegged or adjustable rate systems. The options favored currently are currency boards and unions (Dornbusch) and floating exchange rates (Eichengreen), even though

---

[4] Calvo (1998) and Williamson (1996, 2000) provide some objections to the new consensus. Calvo (2000b) discusses the case for a hard peg. See Kenen (2001, chapter 3) for an excellent overview and critical discussion of recent arguments concerning exchange rate regimes. Much of the literature on exchange rate regimes has a normative bend (should countries adopt fixed or flexible rates?). Less has been written about how countries actually select an exchange rate regime. Tornell and Velasco (2000) build on the standard view that, when government spending can be accommodated through seignorage, fixed rates impose more fiscal discipline as lax fiscal policies eventually lead to an exhaustion of reserves and an end to the peg. In their model, the inflation tax burden associated with a lax fiscal policy is spread over time under a flexible rate instead of pushed into the future as under a fixed rate. This may offer one perspective as to why fixed rates are adopted.

[5] Hard pegs refer to fixing the exchange rate to a hard currency and holding enough reserves (say, equal to the monetary base) to back up the peg.

many countries still prefer to manage their exchange rates. It is clear, though, that countrywide crises, be they triggered by poor domestic policies, a jump in the oil price, a sharp drop in a commodity price, a change in international interest rates, increased trade competition, or a foreign recession, will still exist regardless of the exchange rate regime.

A critique

There is no denying that steps in the direction defined by the pillars of the consensus view would reduce a country's risk of crisis and thereby reassure foreign investors. The consensus view raises some hard questions, though:

- First, that of the objective function: Preventing crises cannot be a goal in itself; after all, prohibiting foreign borrowing would eliminate the threat of foreign debt crisis altogether! The question therefore is, how desirable are those policies when trying to accomplish a well-stated, unambiguous objective? This leads one to question the first two pillars concerning dangerous forms of finance. There is a nagging suspicion that one may be addressing the *symptoms* and ignoring the fundamentals. As Jeanne (2000) argues with regards to currency and maturity mismatches,

> It is difficult to assess the relative merits of these reforms, however, without understanding the underlying reasons why mismatches arise in the balance sheet of emerging countries.

The reform proposals aimed at eliminating dangerous forms of finance may well be misleading if they are based solely on the consideration of the ex post (crisis time) effect of mismatches and ignore both their private rationale and their social impact on ex ante (pre-crisis) government incentives.

For example, as argued by Jeanne (1998, 2000) and Kashyap (1999), short-term debt is a natural reaction to the uncertainty faced by foreign creditors with respect to eventual repayment.[6] Keeping an exit option is a standard protection for creditors against abuse by the debtor. Jeanne (2000) builds an interesting model of the maturity mismatch in which the benefit of short-term debt over long-term debt is that the threat of a fundamental-based run induces the government to implement a fiscal adjustment[7]. The cost is the possibility of a non- fundamental-based run. He studies the impact of various proposals in the context of his model and shows, for example, that taxing short-term debt flows is unambiguously welfare-decreasing. This illustrates the importance of looking also at fundamentals and not simply at symptoms.

The possibility that we are treating the symptoms suggests that we ought to return to first principles.

• Second, and assuming that they are indeed desirable, one may ask, why were those great policies not adopted earlier, and if some obstacle has to be removed, how will they come about in the future? That is, the consensus view must address the question of why the sure-fire recipes failed to be implemented. In this respect, it faces a difficult choice between two hypotheses:

– *Government incompetence.* According to this hypothesis, the proposed reforms were never put in place because the country's politicians and bureaucrats

---

[6] To be certain, some of the maturity mismatch is policy induced; for example, Korea discriminated against long-term foreign investment. But there is no doubt that the main reason for the maturity mismatch is investors' concerns.

[7] In the same way short-term debt constrains misbehavior by an ordinary corporation: see, e.g., Calomiris–Kahn (1991), Jensen (1986), and Rey–Stiglitz (1994).

were utterly incompetent. While this has probably been the case in some instances, I would not take this hypothesis too seriously, at least not as universal. First, governments often pretend not to hear international advice when the latter conflicts with their political interest. Second, under the incompetence hypothesis, the IMF and other IFIs would have a remarkably straightforward job: their experts would simply have to evangelize the consensus view among politicians and bureaucrats (perhaps in private, as the latter may not want to admit incompetence). The country's politicians and bureaucrats would then embrace and obediently follow the advice. The hypothesis in this respect seems counter to what one would expect to happen.

- *Political economy.* According to this hypothesis, the proposed policies were never implemented because it was not in the interest of the governments to do so. While this is my favorite hypothesis of the two, it is not, *as it stands*, without difficulties. It suggests that, to have any content, such policies should be *imposed* by foreigners upon a country and its legitimately elected government. Such a paternalistic attitude conflicts with much of the economic experts' proper concern about country ownership and the widespread criticisms of IMF arrogance.

Conflicting advice and the topsy-turvy principle

While reaching a consensus view on the seven pillars, economists disagree on many other issues. Let me help explain why they do [and why they may keep on disagreeing until an *empirical* consensus is reached]. At an abstract level, the conflicting advice stems from a key *trade-off between ex ante (pre crisis) incentives and ex post efficiency (satisfactory crisis resolution).* Orderly workouts may conflict with the incentives of countries and investors to avoid crises. In other words, confidence is often the mirror image of moral hazard.

At the risk of oversimplifying, for each issue I shall divide economic experts into those who stress ex ante borrower and lender incentives, and those who aim at efficient crises resolutions (individual positions vary with the issue). The former (let's call them "hawks" for convenience) focus on deterrence and recommend tough sanctions against countries that misbehave and international investors who overlend. Arguing that crises won't fail to occur anyway, the latter (the "doves") are more concerned about an orderly workout of the crises.

The topsy-turvy principle states that for policies of interest, there is an inherent conflict between ex ante incentives and ex post efficiency. There is nothing mysterious in this conflict, which is faced by ordinary corporations when designing a financing scheme and a corporate governance framework. Let us illustrate it through a few issues.

• *IMF liquidity provision.* The IMF has moved in the direction of a lender of last resort (LOLR) by adopting, in 1997, an emergency financing mechanism to speed disbursement, and by extending its ability to lend into arrears (that is, to lend to a country that is in arrears to private creditors and has not yet renegotiated these private debts).[8] This move is consistent

---

[8] In 1998, the IMF modified its 1989 policy allowing the Fund to lend to members after sovereign arrears to commercial banks have emerged but before agreements to restructure such debts have been reached. The 1998 modification extends the policy to cover sovereign arrears to other (nonbank) creditors, and to nonsovereign arrears to private creditors arising from the imposition of exchange controls.

with the advice of the many economists who are dovish on this issue.[9]

The hawks, e.g. Schwartz (1999), resolutely oppose the LOLR function on the basis that it encourages countries (or investors) to overborrow (or overlend). Others formally endorse the LOLR function, but qualify this endorsement through various restrictions. For example, the Meltzer Commission (2000) recommends that IMF loans have a short maturity (typically a few months), pay a penalty rate, be senior to all debts and be secured by government bonds. There are, of course, limits as to what such loans can achieve. As is the case for banks, for which discount window lending at penalty rates or deposit insurance premia indexed on capital adequacy would aggravate difficulties and exacerbate moral hazard,[10] penalty-rate emergency loans, while providing better ex ante incentives than penalty-free emergency loans, also conflict with an ex post efficient resolution of the crisis. Furthermore, liquidity loans, almost by definition, cannot be fully secured. Real assets that are used to secure the liquidity loans, thereby making them almost riskless, cannot be employed to attract alternative forms of financing. In other words, secured liquidity loans crowd out other forms of liquidity.

• *IMF conditionality.* The concept of conditionality has recently been extended to encompass a broad array of macroeconomic policies and institutions.

The doves in the matter, a group of critics on the left and right, argue that IMF policies are too intrusive (Feld-

---

[9] E.g., Allen–Gale (2000a), Chang (1999), Eichengreen (1999), Fischer (1999a, b), Krugman (1999a), Obstfeld (2000), Sachs (1998).

[10] See Dewatripont–Tirole (1994a) for a formal analysis of the incentives provided by such policies.

stein 1998[11]), do not reflect country ownership, and hurt the poor (Meltzer Commission 2000) or are unnecessarily constraining (Stiglitz).[12]

• *Capital controls.* Economists' conventional wisdom in the matter of capital controls has until recently been that financial integration is beneficial to the host country and that capital controls, besides not always being effective, are welfare-reducing. The primary argument behind this broad consensus is that the host country can tap international sources of finance to fund its development and to diversify the country risk. It is also been argued that foreign investment promotes the development of domestic financial markets and that FDI brings know-how to the domestic industry.

This consensus has been shattered lately. While Summers (2000) calls for the elimination of biaises[13] that lead to an excessive accumulation of short-term debt and argues that controls of short-term flows tend to be ineffective over time and discourage the integration of financial services that can be an important source of stability, several other prominent economists have advocated direct or indirect restrictions on capital flows. Baghwati (1998) argues that the benefits from financial integration apply only to long-term direct investment. Krugman (1998) proposes curfews on capital outflows. Proponents of controls on short-term capital inflows include Sachs–Woo (2000), Eichengreen (1999, in

[11] Feldstein argues that the IMF attitude in Asia showed much arrogance and usurped sovereign responsibilities.

[12] The IMF has also been severely criticized for its time-inconsistency. As already discussed, some of the tough policies imposed on Asian countries (e.g., the fiscal targets) were quickly relaxed.

[13] Restrictions on foreign direct investment or on access by nonresidents to long-term bond markets, and tax incentives that favor debt over equity instruments.

favor of Chilean-style[14] taxes on short-term capital inflows), and Caballero (2000, who argues that taxing capital inflows contingently, i.e., removing the taxes during external distress, may be justified).[15]

Leaving aside the technical question of whether capital controls are indeed effective or can be evaded through various schemes,[16] as well as the possibility that capital controls may engender corruption, most would agree that taxing short-term foreign investments both reduces ex post the probability of a crisis and makes it harder ex ante for the country to access capital, as there is a reason why investors are unwilling to lend long in the first place.

A similar point applies to the proposal of IMF-sanctioned standstill, or to proposals encouraging suspensions of convertibility.[17] A couple of recent proposals[18] have pushed for "Chapter 11"-style petitions for debt relief.[19]

---

[14] Chilean-style unremunerated reserve requirements (which were abandoned in Chile in 1998) impose a tax on short-term capital inflows. From 1992 through 1998, 30 percent of inflows had to be deposited at no interest at the Chilean central bank for a one-year period. The shorter the maturity, therefore, the larger the tax.

[15] Similarly, a report from a group sponsored by America's Council on Foreign Relations (including Bergsten, Eichengreen, Feldstein, Goldstein, Krugman, Soros, and Volcker) recommended the use of a holding tax on short-term capital inflows for countries with weak financial systems.

[16] One issue is that domestic agents can enter offshore swap contracts with foreign holders of (what resembles) long-term debt. See Garber (1998) for a good account of possible schemes that can be designed to evade capital controls.

[17] Remember for instance that convertibility of short-term loans to Korea was suspended in December 1997.

[18] E.g., Schwarcz (2000).

[19] In reference to the US bankruptcy law. Under Chapter 11 bankruptcy, the firm files for bankruptcy but continues to operate under the same management. Management designs and proposes a reorganization plan that specifies how claims on the firm are altered or compensated (e.g., debt-equity swaps, debt forgiveness, etc.). The reorganization must be approved by a majority of shareholders and a majority of each class of creditors.

- *Orderly workouts.* The doves in the matter include Eichengreen and Portes (1995, 1997, see also Portes 2000) who have argued in favor of creditor committees.[20] The general idea is to facilitate renegotiation of foreign debt so as to avoid inefficient liquidations in situations of foreign distress. Loan contracts would be rewritten in order to clarify the representation of creditors by introducing a collective representation clause for sovereign bond agreements and to permit a qualified majority vote to restructure lending terms.[21] The orderly workout would then be enabled by the IMF lending into arrears, that is, providing finance to the country even when the latter is in arrears to private creditors.

As is well-known, bond issues are as a rule harder to renegotiate than commercial syndicated bank loans, which involve many fewer creditors. Many sovereign bonded debt agreements are written under State of New York law.[22] Renegotiation is not facilitated by this statute, which does not include contractual provisions for qualified majorities to modify the terms of the bonds and to impose such modifications on minority bondholders. The unanimity requirement provides incentives for minorities to disrupt the renegotiation

[20] The Eichengreen–Portes proposal has been very influential in policy circles. In 1996, the Rey committee recommended the use of collective action clauses to facilitate the restructuring of bonded debt. The proposal was also received favorably in various fora such as the G-7 and by the IMF.

[21] Along these lines, the G-10 (1996) suggested including majority voting, sharing of haircuts, and non-acceleration clauses for sovereign bonds. The G-22 (1998) took a similar stance on the issue. On April 21, 1999, Rubin, then US Secretary of the Treasury, argued strongly in favor of such covenants. Eichengreen–Portes (1997) and De Gregorio et al (1999) argue that the potential for negative signaling by countries adopting such provisions can be undone by instructing the Fund to lend at more attractive rates to countries that issue debt securities with such provisions.

[22] See the 1999 IMF note on "The IMF Policy on Lending into Arrears to Private Creditors" for more detail.

process to enable them to obtain a favorable settlement from the debtor or to be bought out by other creditors. Bonds governed by UK law, by contrast, include provisions that make it easy to call a bondholders meeting and empower a qualified majority at the meeting to make deals that are binding on the minority as well.

Doves in the matter also include proponents of an IMF acting as a coordinator of crisis resolution (e.g., Feldstein 1998, Fischer 1999).

Hawks in the matter include investment professionals who are worried that a greater ability to renegotiate debts in a distress contingency makes it more likely that this contingency will arise in the future.[23] Roubini (2000) studies recent bond restructurings in Pakistan, Ukraine, Russia, and Ecuador; these restructurings occurred through debt exchange offers and, in the case of Russia and Ecuador, there were no collective action clauses. He argues that collective action clauses have played a minor role. While pointing out that exchange offers are facilitated by the presence of collective action clauses that bind-in holdouts, Roubini expresses concern about the possibility that structured renegotiation would prove too bureaucratic.

[23] For example in Jeanne's (2000) theoretical model, the institution of a creditor committee to renegotiate sovereign debt reduces the cost of a crisis and has two effects: a beneficial one (reduction in the cost of unavoidable runs) and an adverse incentive one. Jeanne correctly argues that one should make a distinction between renegotiation-friendly measures, such as the institution of a creditor committee, which facilitates an orderly workout, and borrower-friendly measures, which shift the bargaining power in the renegotiation towards the borrower. The adverse incentive effect disappears if the borrower has little bargaining power. While it is straightforward to facilitate renegotiation through institutional design, it is less easy simultaneously to facilitate renegotiation and create a low bargaining power for the borrower. More research on this topic is warranted.

"Unrealistic" encroachments on sovereignty

Arguing that a country's governments and institutions
are not to be trusted, a number of economists have
suggested that key sovereign control rights should be
transferred to new supranational institutions. Cooper
(1984) proposes the creation of a world currency and
Central Bank; Sachs (1995), that of an international
bankruptcy court; Kaufman (1998), Krugman, Eatwell,
and Taylor, the creation of a world financial regulator;
and Soros, that of an International Central Bank acting
as lender of last resort.

While I concur with Eichengreen (1999, 2000, who
calls them "pie-in-the-sky-schemes") that such reforms
are rather unrealistic at this stage, I also feel that we
should listen to visionaries, as some previously unthink-
able transfers of power to supranational authorities have
occurred in the past. Still, such schemes should be
analyzed in a broader context and not solely as a patch
to existing foreign debt crises. In particular, they should
be assessed in the light of recent and future work in
political economy on the optimal size of countries and
degree of subsidiarity.

Theories

There are currently two broad perspectives on EM
crises,[24] with very different policy implications: the
"fundamental" and the "panic" views.

---

[24] Good discussions of the theories can be found, e.g., in Corsetti (1999) and
Eichengreen (1999).

"Fundamental" view

The fundamental view, perhaps developed most forcefully by Corsetti–Pesenti–Roubini (1999) and Burnside–Eichenbaum–Rebello (1999, 2000, 2001), traces crises to fundamental weaknesses in a country's economy. It builds on and extends the traditional (e.g., Krugman's 1979) view that balance-of-payments crises are driven by poor fundamentals (current account and fiscal deficits associated with terms of trade shocks, investment distortions or institutional and political weaknesses). However, this old-style perspective was widely perceived to be an inadequate explanation for recent crises. The fundamentals in East Asia, for example, appeared very solid: no or low budget deficits, reasonable levels of public debt, low inflation, high savings rates.

The fundamental view argues that appearances are deceiving. In this case, the financial sector's low capitalization and poor risk management exposed governments to large implicit liabilities. When East Asia was exposed to several shocks in the mid-1990s (increasing competition of Chinese exports, recession in Japan, appreciation of the dollar after 1995), leading to further financial difficulties, and foreign investors became aware of the gravity of the situation, capital flows quickly reversed.

The strength of the fundamental perspective is that it builds on well-documented banking fragility and implicit guarantees given by governments to domestic and foreign depositors. It makes a coherent argument that the currencies of crisis countries had to depreciate in order to reflect the fundamentals.

What the fundamental view implies for the IMF and other IFIs is less clear. If we accept that sovereign authority should be respected, the fact that some governments (e.g., Mexico in 1995, Asian countries), possibly because of crony capitalism, left their countries with huge tax bills and widespread recessions should not be a motive for intervention, however shocking the outcome. After all, the US government's mishandling of the S&L crisis in the 1980s or the French Credit Lyonnais scandal (albeit with smaller consequences in relative terms) have always been viewed as internal matters, of concern primarily to domestic voters.

It is sometimes argued that things are different in the case of EM crises, since so much money at stake is owned by foreigners. This point, however, requires further elaboration. After all, these foreign investors lend willingly, and are not directly hurt by the EM taxpayers' (involuntary) guarantee of bank deposits. In contrast, the international community may be hurt if the IMF or creditor countries' governments are drawn into debtor country bailouts. Such an expectation of an international bailout – the "moral hazard play" – seems to have been widespread in the case of Russia in 1998 (these expectations failed to be realized, as it turned out). If the creditors and the debtor stall in their negotiation, creditor countries' governments, to the extent that they enjoy large gains from trade with the debtor country or have geopolitical stakes in the country's stability, may be drawn into contributing to rescheduling agreements (Bulow–Rogoff 1988, 1989). In the presence of such "ex post subsidies", competitive lenders are willing to lend more at any given interest rate and the borrowing country is able to extract the corresponding surplus.

The amounts lent by the official sector, however, while huge by historical standards, have remained limited relative to the size of recent crises. Furthermore, they have received preferred creditor status.[25] Indeed, there is little evidence that international transfers associated with big international bailouts are commensurate with the domestic internal transfers. Summers (2000) argues that this is unlikely for recent crises. Brealey (1999) similarly views the danger of moral hazard created by the prospect of IMF assistance as often overstated:

> The subsidy in IMF loans is negligible compared with the losses that have been suffered by investors in East Asia, Russia and Brazil.

Jeanne and Zettelmeyer (2000, 2001) provide some empirical evidence to this effect. Because the direct losses incurred by official lenders in big international bailouts may underestimate the true losses (some loans are rolled over), they look at the "most pessimistic scenario" in which currently existing IMF claims are worthless. They find that IMF lending subsidies are quite small and that it is the domestic

---

[25] As Roubini (2000, p26) points out: "The simplistic idea that a sovereign would follow reckless policies that lead to financial distress for the country in order to end up receiving IMF assistance does not make too much sense. First, such policies are highly costly, in terms of output, inflation and other welfare measures; second, sovereigns tend to resist the idea of asking for IMF support as it is perceived to be costly; third, IMF assistance comes with strings, conditionality and is subject to often painful adjustment policies. On the other hand, it is also true that, while a sovereign may not purposely follow reckless policies to get IMF support, its policies may at the margin be biased towards risky and unsound behavior if there is some expectation of external financial support in case of trouble." The expectation of an external bailout may nevertheless play a role in the case of large countries – with systemic consequences such as in the case of Russia, which was deemed to be "too nuclear to fail".

taxpayer, not the global taxpayer, who ultimately foots the bill.[26]

Discussion: What is "moral hazard"? Where is the body? I have eschewed the use of "moral hazard" even though the "fundamental view" is sometimes also called the "moral hazard view". The problem is that the literature has given different meanings to "moral hazard", and these meanings have sharply different policy implications. Let us therefore try to sort out the different interpretations.

The first and most frequent interpretation refers to moral hazard on the part of the host country's government's. The fundamental view's starting point – that the government accumulates substantial implicit liabilities through lax banking supervision – refers to an important form of government moral hazard. The granting of implicit or explicit government guarantees leading to overborrowing by domestic agents is accordingly often referred to as "debtor moral hazard" in commentaries.[27] As we will discuss in Chapter 5, there are many other relevant forms of government moral hazard, with different implications.

---

[26] "Based on the historical record, an EMBIG economy [country belonging to J.P. Morgan's "EMBI Global" Index, a group of 27 relatively advanced emerging countries] that borrows 10 percent of its GDP would fail to repay with a probability of at most 5 percent – the probability of an "infinite cycle" for this class of countries. The resulting implicit transfer – due to the fact that the interest rate charged by the IMF fails to reflect this default risk – is thus less than 0.5 percent of the country's GDP. If the country represents 1 percent of the world population and GDP (this corresponds to a large emerging economy, between Argentina and Brazil in size), the per capita cost of the bailout for the global taxpayer would amount to less than 0.0005 times that borne by the domestic taxpayer. It bears emphasizing that even these small numbers are based on an extreme assumption underpinning our hypothetical worst case scenario, namely, that none of the outstanding debt on "infinite" lending cycles will be recovered. Thus, a reasonable estimate of the ex ante subsidy implicit in IMF lending is likely to be much smaller."

[27] See, e.g., Calvo (2000b) and Roubini (2000).

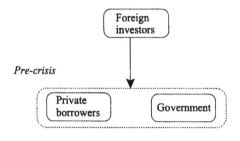

Pre-crisis

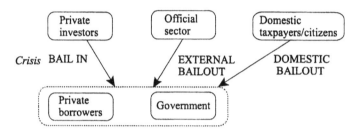

Crisis

Figure 3.   Burden Sharing

In the fundamental view, the domestic taxpayer foots the bill. More generally, a key determinant of incentives is, as is widely recognized in commentaries, who shares the burden. Roughly, there are three possible victims: the domestic taxpayers, the foreign investors whose equity value is depreciated or debt claim is in default or renegotiated, and the "official sector" (which we define here as IFIs plus advanced countries' Treasuries) that can lose money in attempting rescues: see Figure 3.

As we have seen, the burden sometimes falls entirely on domestic taxpayers, as in Mexico in 1995.[28] Most

---

[28] A number of observers argue that the IMF creates moral hazard even if its loans are repaid. According to this view, the IMF enables the country's government, captured by borrowers, to shift the losses from borrowers and lenders to the local taxpayer by providing a bridge loan.

often, however, it is shared between domestic taxpayers and foreign investors. The latter suffer through the loss of value of their equity portfolios, through default of debt claims, or through renegotiation of these claims via private sector involvement (PSI). Despite many claims concerning bailouts by the IMF and the US government,[29] external bailouts have been relatively limited, as we discussed earlier. Certainly, the fact that most loans have been repaid in itself does not mean that the large-scale rescue attempts were not external bailouts, because such loans may have been very risky at the time they were issued. In any case, with the ever-escalating size of official loans, we cannot dismiss the possibility of future external bailouts.

The concept of "creditor moral hazard", although often employed, is more delicate. Roughly, it has two meanings: overlending in the pre-crisis stage, and attempting to shift the burden (extract bailout money from the official sector or the domestic taxpayer) in the case of a crisis. Even assuming that investors invest in expectation that official or taxpayer resources will be available for bailouts, the notion of overlending moral hazard (also called the "moral hazard play" in commentaries) – the market bets on a rescue – is, as its stands, puzzling. Investors are motivated by profit and react to the incentives given to them. Foreign investors may well be very happy to lend to weak banks and firms, knowing that the latter will be rescued by an external or internal bailout. Blaming investors for reacting mechanically to incentives distorted by the host government and/or the official sector is really an attempt by the latter to deny

---

[29] For example, it is often argued that the IMF and the US Treasury bailed out Mexico in 1995. This is an improper use of the term, unless clear evidence is supplied for the thesis that the official sector's loans were unlikely to be repaid and that the official sector was just lucky.

their responsibilities.[30] The issue of investors' strategies to shift the burden during a crisis in contrast deserves more attention.

Remark: other fundamentalist theories. While the dominant "fundamental view" emphasizes government bailouts, Caballero and Krishnamurthy (2001b) stress private sector fundamentals as the culprit for inefficient crises. Their starting point is the important question of whether and why private domestic borrowers underinsure against country shocks and exchange rate depreciation by contracting dollar-denominated debt. Foreign-currency-denominated debt implies that those firms whose assets are in domestic currency suffer grave liquidity shocks when the currrency depreciates. Caballero and Krishnamurthy show that firms have no incentive to underinsure if domestic financial markets are well developed, but that they will contract excessively foreign-currency-denominated debt if domestic financial markets are inefficient.[31] The outcome is an overreaction to country-specific shocks in countries with domestic financial underdevelopment.

---

[30] For bank loans, a case can be made that foreign creditors do not only commit their own money, but also that of their home countries, since the lending banks may need to be rescued by taxpayer funds after losing money in crisis countries. To a large extent, however, this problem is of concern primarily to the advanced countries' supervisory authorities and deposit insurance funds. There is not that much difference between Credit Lyonnais' investing in frail-looking companies and its lending to crisis-prone developing countries. In both cases, the French taxpayers foot the bill.

[31] In contrast, Burnside et al (2001) argue that it is government guarantees that make it optimal for banks to have an unhedged currency mismatch between their assets and their liabilities.

"Panic" or "multiple equilibria" view

A number of economists (e.g., Calomiris 1999, Cole–
Kehoe 1998, Chang–Velasco 1999, Feldstein 1998,
Masson 1999a,b, Obstfeld 2000, Sachs 1998) have
used an analogy with bank runs to analyze recent
crises. Bank runs may arise when short-term cred-
itors/depositors start refusing to roll over their claims
on the banks and demand immediate payment. The
bank, which performs a maturity transformation function and has longer maturities on the asset side, is then
forced to liquidate some long-term assets at a cost,
making other creditors/depositors worried that they
will not be able to recoup their investment, thereby
inducing them to run for the exit. The eventual
outcome may well be socially inefficient. In particular,
creditors collectively would be better off if each
(hypothetically) could commit to roll over any claims
unless they individually really need the money. By
analogy, many economists have argued that foreign
investors may scramble for exits out of the country
before others do and that this behavior, while individually rational, is collectively irrational and, furthermore, hurts the borrowing country:

> There is no 'fundamental' reason for Asia's financial
> calamity except financial panic itself... Asia is reeling
> not from a crisis of fundamentals, but from a self-fulfill-
> ing withdrawal of short-term loans, one that is fuelled by
> each investor's recognition that all other investors are
> withdrawing their claims. Since short-term debts exceed
> foreign exchange reserves, it is 'rational' for each inves-
> tor to join the panic (Sachs, 1997).

In this basic story, as in the original bank-run models of
Bryant (1980) and Diamond–Dybvig (1983), the panic
outcome is *one* possible outcome (if other depositors do

not panic, I have no reason to panic). The panic view has therefore been criticized as lacking predictive power.[32] Recently, though, richer models have been developed that may predict unique outcomes (panic or no panic): see Morris–Shin (1998) and Rochet–Vives (2000).

When compared with the fundamental view, the panic view leads to quite different implications. As fundamental imbalances are not the cause of the crisis, policy tightening may do more harm (i.e., exacerbate the crisis) than good. Rather, the panic view leads to the conclusion that crises should be prevented either by avoiding dangerous forms of debt, or through access to a credit facility, or both. Many instruments can be used for this purpose:

- capital controls (e.g., controls on capital outflows to eliminate the panic, reserve requirements to limit short-term foreign borrowing)
- elimination of currency and maturity mismatches in foreign borrowing
- IMF-sanctioned standstills (debt service suspensions, suspension of convertibility) or debt-equity swaps, and
- credit line available either from the IMF or from large private financial institutions (as in the case of Argentina and Mexico).

---

[32] Some proponents of the panic view actually regard this lack of predictive power as a strength of the theory since the recent crises were poorly foreseen by observers. On the other hand, the fundamental view and other views may be consistent with poorly foreseen crises as the countrywide exposures are hard to measure, as we will later argue. Furthermore, one cannot exclude that advances in our theoretical and empirical knowledge of the functioning of this new breed of crises will make them easier to forecast. It should also be noted that runs-based approaches may be combined with fundamentals-based theories. Crises are then driven partly by weak fundamentals and partly by runs. An illustration of this mixed approach is provided by Chari–Kehoe (2001), in which foreign investors receive private signals about country strength and engage in (privately rational) herd behavior.

With so many instruments available, it is hard to see how a crisis could occur. The panic view, therefore, is somewhat incomplete as it does not account for the feasible institutional responses to the underlying problem. The fact that the "anti-run devices" are not always in place suggests that there are deeper political and economic forces in play that must be accounted for before we can draw with confidence the policy implications of the panic view. The panic view, as it stands in the narratives, does not account well for the existence of crises and therefore does not yet provide a firm foundation on which to base policy recommendations. My "gut feeling", though, is that it is well worth pursuing research in this direction. Indeed the panic view is useful as a sensible-looking building block to describe what may happen in specific circumstances, and (in those versions of the theory predicting a unique outcome) to analyze the timing and dynamics of the crisis.

3

Outline of the Argument and Main Message

The discussion in Chapter 2 is shadowed by a lingering question: What are we trying to do? Preventing crises is not a goal in itself; after all, prohibiting foreign borrowing would eliminate the threat of foreign debt crisis altogether! The issue therefore is, how desirable are specific policies when trying to accomplish a well-stated, unambiguous objective?

In this respect, I am struck by the fact that proposals for a new international financial architecture rarely formulate a clear objective function. Or else, and almost equivalently, they offer a whole array of objectives: avoid financial crises, resolve them in an orderly manner, economize on taxpayer money, protect foreign investors, respect country sovereignty, limit output volatility, prevent contagion, facilitate the country's access to funds, promote long-term growth, and force structural reforms – to which can be added the IMF's traditional current account, international reserves, and inflation objectives. There are just too many goals, not to mention the fact that many of them are conflicting! Clearly, we need to go back to fundamentals and identify the market failures, if any, that underlie the existence of IFIs.

Let us begin our theoretical treatment with the architecture of the argument and relegate the details to the subsequent chapters.

The problem of a standard borrower

Going back to basics leads us to revisit the obvious point that the unit of analysis is the relationship between a "borrower" (the debtor country) and a "lender" (the international financial community).

To secure funds, a borrower needs to put in place rules of behavior, that will apply both before and after the uncertainty is resolved. Financing arrangements have to resolve the basic problem of reassuring investors about the prospect of recouping their investment. In so doing, they need to strike a balance between the costs and benefits of alternative financing and governance institutions (allocating control and cash flow rights, defining a monitoring structure, liquidity and risk management, bankruptcy and workout procedures).

Investor protection benefits the borrower more than the investors, as long as the latter compete for the borrower's business.

Why is external borrowing different?

The need to put in place financing arrangements that reassure investors about the prospect of recouping their investment exists at both the domestic and international level. What makes the latter special is the presence of a "third player", the borrower's government, who shares with the private domestic borrowers the control rights not vested with investors, who is able to heavily influence the return effectively obtained by the investors, and with whom investors do not contract. Because the investors' return is affected by the behavior of two agents, the borrower himself and its government, I call this the *dual-agency problem* (Figure 4).

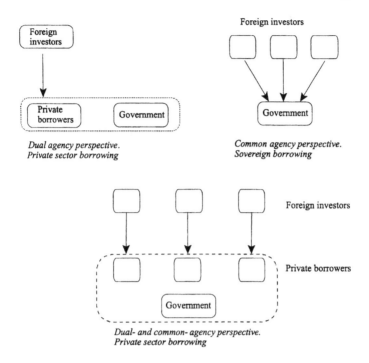

Figure 4.

The government has both the *incentives* and the *means* not to fully protect the foreign investors. Governments do not derive any more utility from lowering the return on foreign investments than homeowners do from setting fire to their house once insured. They do not per se enjoy devaluing the claims of foreigners and mostly do not do it willingly. Rather, they are less cautious than they should be at the margin; they will not take any action that reduces the probability of a crisis if it entails a substantial political cost.

Incentives to favor, at the margin, domestic constituencies over foreign investors are provided either by democratic accountability, that induces governments to pander to domestic political constituencies, or by conflicts of interest and capture, that induce politicians to favor specific interest groups. The means are the extensive control rights held by governments. These are much more important in an international context than domestically, since a myriad of government actions affect the exchange rate and, more generally, the returns enjoyed by foreign investors.

The same conjunction of large discretionary powers and biased incentives engenders a second key difference between domestic corporate borrowing and international borrowing: the *common agency problem*, which applies directly to sovereign borrowing, and indirectly (through the dual agency problem) to private borrowing as well. When several lenders lend to a single borrower, each lender takes no account of the impact of its lending and associated contractual provisions on the other lenders. This lending externality is present in corporate borrowing, with the presence of a large number of equityholders, of bondholders, and of multiple securities. But some of the responses to this common agency problem that have been designed in the corporate context, have no natural counterpart in the international context.

Institutional and policy responses to market failure

Financial arrangements at the international level are improved if some institution (the IMF, say) acts as a delegated monitor on behalf of investors and is able to contract with the government, thus "re-balancing" the dual- and the common-agency problems, ultimately to the benefit of the borrowing country.

This perspective provides a conceptual framework in which to assess the current proposals for redesigning the international financial architecture and identifies the motivation for refocusing the IMF. The framework internalizes the reasons why some features of existing financial arrangements are present in the first place, thus avoiding the risk of merely treating the symptoms, and considers the impact of privately optimal financial arrangements on a government's incentives and behavior. The absence of incentive in individual lending relationships to constrain government moral hazard has a number of nonstandard, but intuitive implications.

4

Liquidity and Risk-Management in a Closed Economy

A central question addressed in this book is the extent to which a country resembles or differs from an ordinary borrower. To set the stage, we therefore need to recap the main features of financing agreements. My coverage of corporate financing will be sketchy and highly selective, and will focus on the themes that are most relevant to the subsequent chapters. For obvious reasons, I will put special emphasis on control rights and liquidity and risk management issues. I will then discuss the notion and the role of domestic liquidity[1] before turning to the international context in the next chapter.

Corporate financing: key organizing principles

Corporate finance refers to the set of institutions and policies that make it credible that the suppliers of funds to a firm will recoup their investment, and thereby make it possible for the borrower to have access to funds in the first place. Corporate finance is therefore about harnessing income that can be pledged to investors.

From this perspective, all institutions and practices of corporate financing, solvency ratios, liquidity require-

---

[1] The reader is referred to Holmström–Tirole (2001b) for a broader treatment of the themes developed in this chapter.

ments, lines of credit, duration analysis, currency matching, corporate governance, and bankruptcy processes, have a common rationale. They all reflect the existence of a wedge between the total value generated by the productive activity and the smaller amount that can be credibly promised to outside investors, what we will call for lack of a better term "pledgeable income". This *wedge between value and pledgeable income* is due to two factors or types of nonpledgeable income. First, insiders derive private benefits from their position (employment, prestige, perks, etc.) that cannot be appropriated by the firm's financiers. Second, insiders may need to be provided with financial incentives if their policy preferences are to be somewhat aligned with those of the investors; without such financial incentives, they may engage in pet projects and build empires, pay insufficient attention to subcontracting or labor costs, overlook their employees' risk management procedures, allocate too little time to their position by overcommitting themselves with competing activities (boards of directors, political activism, investments in other ventures), enjoy excessive perks, favor their friends, or engage in a wide variety of self-dealing behaviors. In a nutshell, and from the investors' viewpoint, they may "misbehave".

That the outside investors cannot (and actually may not want to) appropriate the full value is the essence of credit rationing – the fact that some socially desirable projects do not receive funding from capital markets – but it has much broader implications.[2]

---

[2] We will couch our discussion mainly in terms of borrower incentives. Adverse selection – the possibility that the borrower is better informed than the investors at the contracting stage – and the concomitant screening issues are also important, as documented for example by Kaplan–Strömberg (2000); with a few exceptions, they lead to conclusions that are similar to the moral hazard/incentive approach discussed here.

To have access to funds, firms need to take steps to reassure the investors as to the prospect of recouping their investment. A first point worth noting is that investor protection is not so much about protecting investors as about benefitting borrowers. Investor protection is about enabling borrowers to have access to funds. Indeed, for given market conditions and with competitive capital markets, a more credible promise of returns to outside investors translates into a more intense competition to lend to the borrowers; investors are then willing to contribute more funds, lend at lower interest rates, demand less collateral, commit more liquidity, and take fewer control rights. Conversely, poor investor protection results at best in higher rates of interests and tougher conditions,[3] and at worst in the absence of financing.

This basic fact, predicted by theory and corroborated by empirical evidence, does not imply that investors have no incentive to lobby for increased protection. Indeed, they have two reasons to do so. First, increased protection benefits their existing assets from past investments. Second, increased protection boosts new investment and therefore the demand for savings. Increased demand for savings raises equilibrium rates of return in the capital market.

Principle 1 (beneficiaries): With competitive capital markets, borrowers are the direct beneficiaries of increased investor protection, as investors compete away the benefits from protection. Investors benefit

---

[3] In the international context, this theoretical statement is corroborated by empirical evidence showing that despite protracted negotiations and restructurings, the realized return on bonds of defaulted countries has been no lower than the returns on domestic risk-free bonds (see, e.g., Foreman–Peck 1994).

indirectly to the extent that the associated increase in investment raises equilibrium rates of return.

For issues of interest, the steps taken to reassure investors are necessarily costly to firms and reduce the net present value (NPV), or "value" for short from now on. A straightforward analogy is that of an entrepreneur pledging a family house with high sentimental value as collateral to a bank in order to be able to borrow. Pledging the house as collateral boosts the income that is pledged to the investors, the pledgeable income, but because it implies an inefficient transfer of property in the event the entrepreneur fails, the policy destroys value. This inefficiency may be the cost to be paid by the entrepreneur to have access to funding. More generally, we can state:

> ***Principle 2 (pledgeable income – value trade-off):*** *Borrowers face a trade-off between pledgeable income and value.*

While the costly-collateral-pledging example provides the intuition, let us give a few other applications of this principle:

(a) Corporate governance.

Consider, first, the institutions of corporate governance. These institutions involve substantial transaction costs, delays and lack of flexibility in managerial decision-making, disclosure of information that may be useful to competitors, and managerial distraction away from core tasks. Corporate governance is entirely about raising the pledgeable income. The fact that borrowers are willing to incur the corresponding costs is clear evidence of the pledgeable income – value trade-off.

(b) Active and speculative monitoring.

Borrowers can increase pledgeable income by enlisting

monitors. There are two types of such monitors corresponding roughly to Hirschman (1970)'s famous distinction between "voice" and "exit". Active monitors are given control rights to interfere with management and prevent returns-decreasing actions. Active monitors form a disparate group: boards of directors, raiders, large shareholders, venture capitalists, main bank lenders, and so on.

While active monitoring is about improving the firm's future financial performance, speculative monitoring is about measuring the current value of assets to investors. Speculative monitors, also called passive monitors, "take a picture" of the current state of the firm and act upon it. This measurement is useful to reward management (e.g., through stock options), adjust liquidity and access to funds, or trigger covenants. Speculative monitors include stock market analysts, investors in Initial Public Offerings (IPOs), short-run debtholders (who measure the value of assets in place to determine whether they should roll over their debt), and rating agencies.

Both types of monitoring are quite costly to the firm. Yet, many firms pay to be rated, incur substantial costs to be listed publicly, or accept to pay premium returns to a venture capitalist or to a main bank. Again, they sacrifice value to raise pledgeable income.

(c) Control rights.

To be able to borrow, entrepreneurs reluctantly relinquish control rights to investors. How many rights they surrender depends on the strength of their balance sheet. Firms with strong balance sheets (high equity, plenty of collateral, guaranteed income stream, etc.) do not need to give investors substantial control. Usually they borrow from the market, and while bond covenants restrict their freedom, relatively little control is relinquished in the process. Firms with weaker balance sheets borrow from banks and accept stricter covenants. Firms with very weak balance sheets, such as high-tech start-ups (with no initial equity, no collateral, and no guaranteed income stream) go to venture capitalists, to whom they confer substantial control, or become divisions of larger firms in which case they also relinquish a fair amount of control rights. Giving control rights to investors is a way of reassuring them about the prospect of recouping their investment.

Our next two principles focus on the allocation of multiple control rights.

> *Principle 3 (relative demand for control rights): Investors should be optimally endowed with those control rights for which they have the highest relative willingness to pay, that is those rights that enable investors to protect their interests without substantially hurting the borrower.*

This principle follows common sense intuition.[4] Endowing investors with a control right strengthens investor protection and thus boosts the pledgeable income. But the exercise of control by investors also creates negative externalities on insiders, as in the case of the scaling-down of a project or the liquidation of assets by creditors who take control after poor performance. The general rule is that rights should be conferred on investors if investor control would lead to value-enhancing actions (investor control then raises both pledgeable income and total value). The investors also receive some rights for which investor control conflicts with value maximization; these rights are determined on the basis of the relative willingness to pay. How many

---

[4] See Aghion–Tirole (1997) for more detail about the allocation of formal control on the basis of relative willingness to pay for the rights.

such rights are conferred upon investors depends, as we have seen, on the strength of the borrower's balance sheet. To provide a trivial illustration of this principle, the borrower's private life or choice of attire usually has a negligible impact on investor returns, yet is of substantial importance to the borrower; we would therefore expect investors not to take control rights in this respect. Similarly, the top executives' choice of close collaborators often affects their lives much more than they affect investor returns; we would therefore expect much freedom in this respect except in those situations in which the choice of collaborator substantially impacts investor performance and the firm's balance sheet is weak (and indeed, venture capitalists may force technology start-up entrepreneurs to take on business-oriented collaborators). In contrast, one would not expect borrowers to have extensive formal[5] control rights in the matters of long-term investment, payout policies, risk management, or the structuring of executive compensation.

This brings us to the next, equally intuitive principle concerning the temporal evolution of control. It may now be useful to consider a simplified time-line that is often used in financial economics (see Figure 5).

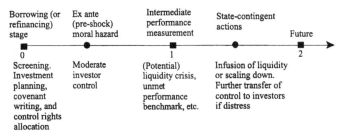

Figure 5.

---

[5] They may still enjoy real control due to their unique access to information. That is, investors often rubberstamp the borrower's proposals for lack of better ideas.

As Figure 5 indicates, financing amounts and conditions should not be cast in stone at the initial financing stage; rather, they should evolve with the information that accrues over time. The time-line introduces an intermediate stage, at which some information about performance (short-term profit, liquidity needs,etc.) accrues. There is borrower moral hazard (scope for wasting investor money) both before the intermediate stage and after.

"Stage 0" is the initial financing stage (later, we will give an alternative interpretation, in which stage 0 is preceded by previous financing arrangements and is a workout stage in which these previous arrangements are renegotiated). At Stage 0, investors assess the strength of the borrower's balance sheet, and together with the borrower elaborate financing and investment plans, write covenants and allocate control rights. "Stage 1" is a stage of intermediate performance assessment. Information accrues at Stage 1 regarding managerial effectiveness between Stage 0 and Stage 1. This performance may relate to current earnings or future prospects. At that stage, and in conformity with the original plan drawn at State 0, refinancing, reinvestment, and the allocation of cash-flow and control rights are reconsidered. Last, "Stage 2" is a short cut or summary for the future.

Principle 4 (conditionality): The allocation of return streams, liquidity and control rights should be made contingent on the evolution of the borrower's balance sheet.

Conditionality obeys a simple incentive, a carrot-and-stick logic. While pledging the family house raises pledgeable income, pledging it only in case of default by the borrower raises the latter's incentives to avoid default. Pledging the house unconditionally (that is, de facto selling it forward) would create more pledgeable income and keep incentives constant because the lenders would receive the house in all states of nature and not only in case of poor performance; but it would do nothing to promote incentives for good performance. Agency considerations thus often dictate that the transfer be made contingent.

In the case of control rights, conditionality serves another purpose besides raising ex ante incentives. It also reflects the fact that the weaker the firm's intermediate-stage balance sheet, the higher the incentive for ex post borrower misbehavior. A borrower with very little equity left in the firm has an incentive either to let go or to gamble for resurrection. Investor protection therefore becomes more important when the balance sheet has deteriorated. The principle of a contingent transfer of control rights therefore obeys a twin rationale.

The conditionality principle is well-illustrated by Kaplan and Strömberg (1999)'s analysis of venture capital financing agreements. They show that the allocation of cash-flow rights and control rights, and the availability of financing, are contractually contingent on observable measures of financial and non-financial performance. The triggering contingencies are defined by observables such as EBIT (earnings before interest and taxes), net worth, completion of the business plan, FDA or patent approval, sale price of securities, product functionality, or the completion of a strategic partnership. Of particular interest for our discussion of control rights (here measured by voting rights, board rights, and liquidation rights – i.e., the right to force the company to repay, say, the venture capitalist's invested funds or to liquidate), the venture capitalist obtains full control if the company performs poorly. In contrast, the entrepreneur obtains more control when the company performs well as the venture capitalist retains cash flow rights and relinquishes control rights.[6]

The key feature of such arrangements is the contingent transfer of control rights. In venture capital deals, venture capitalists usually start with extensive control rights, which they relinquish in a case of good performance. In contrast, and in accordance with our previous discussion, for borrowers with stronger balance sheets, the evolution is more likely to be from moderate investor control to intrusive investor control in a case of poor performance (as depicted in Figure 5). Indeed, a different, but still similar, pattern is observed in corporations, for which the failure to repay debt, or the violation of other covenants, triggers a shift of control from shareholders to debtholders. This shift adversely affects the firm as the debtholders' cash flow rights make them much more conservative in management and investment policies than shareholders.

Last, the use of terminology ("conditionality") is motivated by the alternative interpretation of Figure 5. As noted earlier, one can also think of Stage 0 as a workout stage in which previous claims on the firm are renegotiated. Conditionality may mean, for example, that the continued debt rollover or capital injection is conditioned on the achievement of short- and medium-term performance targets.

Principle 5 (soft budget constraint): The borrower's and the investors' optimal contractual arrangement may not be time-consistent. In order to provide proper ex ante incentives to the borrower, they may

---

[6] An example of a mechanism shifting the allocation of control rights in a state-contingent manner is conversion. For example, if the IPO price exceeds a threshold, then the venture capitalist must convert his claims into shares and relinquish special control rights.

agree on setting tough conditions for the borrower in a case of poor performance, which they may then choose not to apply ex post if indeed the contingency occurs.

For example, and with reference to the time-line depicted in Figure 5, suppose that the firm's observed Stage 1 performance is its Stage 1 profit, and that this profit depends heavily on the borrower's Stage 0 behavior. It may be optimal for the borrower and the investors to agree to liquidate the assets at Stage 1 in a case of poor Stage-1 performance, and this in order to put pressure on the borrower. But suppose that the assets are valuable in operation at Stage 1 in the sense that even the investors' subsequent return (which, remember, is lower than the total value of continuing, as it does not include the insiders' stake) exceeds the assets' liquidation value, and that the borrower is indispensible in order to continue operations. Then the threat of liquidating the assets is not credible as bygones are bygones; both borrower and investors will want to renegotiate the initial agreement to their mutual advantage when the poor-performance contingency occurs. The expectation of such renegotiation, however, undermines ex ante incentives.

Principle 6 (liquidity and risk management): The rationale for liquidity and risk management is the risk of being exposed to credit rationing in the future. The borrower benefits from committing to insuring partially, although not necessarily fully, against the threat of credit rationing.

Firms and banks hoard liquidity in several ways. They hold liquid assets such as government securities or high-grade debentures issued by the private sector. They also secure credit lines with financial institutions. This liquidity does not come for free. High-grade bonds and government securities command low yields, and credit lines involve various costs (commitment fees, compensatory balances). The mere fact that firms and banks are willing to spend the time and incur these monetary costs in securing their future funding in advance is clear evidence that they are concerned that "wait-and-see" financing, which consists in issuing new securities when refinancing needs arise, will not raise sufficient funds. That is, firms and banks purchase costly insurance against the event of future credit rationing.

Risk management obeys the same logic. While liquidity hoarding is about increasing the *level* of future fund availability, risk management is about reducing the *variability* of this funding. The simple rationale for risk management is to insulate the firm's or the bank's operational and reinvestment decisions from risks that it does not control: foreign exchange fluctuations, interest rate risk, death of a key employee, and so forth.[7]

While insurance is desirable, full insurance may not be, for at least two reasons.[8] First, insurance, as usual, is the mirror image of moral hazard. For example, obtaining insurance against short-term profit fluctuations and the concomitant threat of credit rationing is fine if these

[7] Note that neither liquidity provision nor risk management would arise in an Arrow–Debreu framework. In the absence of credit rationing, that is if the entire value were pledgeable to investors, the firm's operational and reinvestment policies would be entirely forward-looking and thus not depend on the firm's income shocks, for example. Similarly, risk management would be unnecessary for the familiar Modigliani–Miller reason. For more details about risk management theory, see Froot et al (1993) and Holmström–Tirole (2000).

[8] A third reason is provided in Holmström–Tirole (2000). Obtaining insurance against aggregate risk, according to standard finance theory (e.g., CAPM), requires paying a risk premium. This premium implies that a firm should not fully insure against aggregate shocks, but instead should take on some of the aggregate risk.

fluctuations are due to contingencies (e.g., macroeconomic) that are outside the firm's control; it may not
be if these fluctuations are heavily dependent on managerial choices. Second, insuring against the firm's reinvestment shocks (as opposed to against the variability of
revenues destined to cover those shocks) is costly in a
situation of credit rationing. To the extent that the
borrower has committed his existing resources at the
initial stage, future refinancing is always borne, one
way or another, by investors. The latter will therefore
question whether there is enough pledgeable income to
vindicate extensive refinancing.[9]

Let us conclude this highly selective review by a
discussion of another theme with an important counterpart in the international context: the multiplicity of
investors and the concomitant potential for externalities
among investors. The multiplicity of claims and clai-
mants in corporations gives rise to a potential common
agency problem, in which the providers of funds to a firm
may not internalize the externalities that their lending
imposes on other providers of funds. That is, investors
individually have no incentive to take into account the
impact of their lending relationship (level and structure
of investment, monitoring, and exercise of control
rights) on the other investors' returns. Such externalities
exist even if investors hold similar claims on the firm,
and new issues arise when claims are heterogeneous.

Figure 6 summarizes the potential inefficiencies that
may occur in the common agency context and the institutional responses that have been devised to handle the
problems. It is worth stressing once again that while the
focus of the analysis is the harm inflicted by individual
investors onto other investors, this harm is ultimately

[9] For more on this point, see, e.g., Holmström–Tirole (1998).

Issue	Contracting externalities	Collective action	Heterogeneity
Potential inefficiency	Inefficient level and structure of lending	Failure to monitor covenants and compliance thereof and to intervene	Externalities in decision making
Institutional response	(On-and off-) balance sheet transparency, limits on borrowing and seniority rules	Representation	Covenants, security design, legal framework,...

Figure 6.   Common agency

borne by the borrower, who, by way of exchange, has to concede better conditions to the investors and may even lose access to the capital market if satisfactory responses cannot be devised.

- *Contracting externalities.* The first type of externality among investors can be labelled "contracting externalities". An analogy with the insurance market may be useful here. It is well known by both insurers and economic theorists (since Pauly 1974) that the prohibition of exclusivity in insurance contracts leads to over-insurance and therefore to insufficient preventative measures being taken by the insuree (who of course ends up paying higher premia and is the ultimate loser). When an insurance company provides the insuree with a little bit more insurance at the margin, the two parties do not internalize the negative externality (lower effort by the insuree) exerted on the other insurers.[10]

---

[10] The theoretical framework for common agency situations was first provided by Bernheim–Whinston (1986a,b) in the case of moral hazard, and by Martimort (1992) and Stole (1991) in the context of adverse selection. See also Bizer–De Marzo (1992). Dixit (1996) applies the common agency paradigm to the study of institutional design. An excellent review of contracting with externalities is Segal (1999).

Similarly, the design of a contractual relationship (at "Stage 0" in Figure 5) between an investor or group of investors usually affects the return earned by other investors in the firm. Consider, for instance, the possibility that the borrower exploits the dispersion among investors to borrow "too much". Intuitively, "overborrowing," or equivalently "overlending", cannot occur as long as each investor can verify that the borrower does not dilute his claim by issuing new securities to other investors. The biggest threat to one's claim, of course, is the issuance of claims that are equally or more senior[11] or else have a shorter maturity. But even claims that are junior to existing ones pose a threat to the latter, as they dilute the borrower's incentives and thereby make him prone to pay less attention or to take private benefits. Contractual externalities may also lead to an inefficient *structure* of lending. The borrower-investor pair does not internalize the benefit brought about by an increase in the maturity of reimbursements for holders of long-term claims on the firm. This may result in excessively short-term debt that drains the firm's liquidity and jeopardizes long-term investments.

In practice, much of the scope for overborrowing is eliminated by two contractual features: covenants imposing limits on the issuance of equally or more senior securities or, more generally, on overall borrowing;[12]

---

[11] Of course, the issuance of junior claims is equally threatening if the courts treat equally claims with different seniorities. For this reason (as well as for the possible impact of more leverage on insiders' incentives), covenants may limit all future debt issuance (including junk bonds). Keeping with the covenants protecting investors against more junior claims, debt contracts also include a series of covenants relative to potential misbehavior by equityholders. These covenants are not about issuance, but rather address distributions to shareholders (e.g., excessive dividends) that might leave debtholders with an empty shell, and asset substitution, i.e., excessive risk taking (e.g., limits on the shift from tangible to intangible assets).

[12] This includes negative pledges, which prohibit the firm from securing assets beyond some level (say, 10 percent).

and acceleration clauses that make due long-term claims in case of default on shorter-maturity ones. Contractual provisions do not fully eliminate overlending, but they seriously reduce its scope.

• *Collective action.* Even the holders of securities in the same class exert externalities on each other unrelated to the level and structure of borrowing. If they are numerous, no one has the incentive to participate in the careful design of financing arrangements[13] and in the subsequent monitoring of the firm's condition and exercising of the control opportunities available to the class of securities. This problem may be particularly acute for dispersed shareholders,and in case of distress, dispersed bondholders or bank depositors.

As in the case of contractual externalities, institutions have evolved over time so as to deal better with the problem of collective action, associated with the incentive to free-ride. It has been tackled in several ways. In the case of corporate bonds, there is little problem as long as the bonds are high-grade (their value is then only mildly sensitive to firm performance); still, even high-grade bonds may default, and two institutions have been designed to reduce the transaction costs associated with renegotiating the bonds: exchange offers, which allow management to design a workout package (usually a debt-equity swap) that must be approved by a qualified majority of bondholders; and bondholder trustees, who represent bondholders in renegotiations. Moving to more "information-intensive representation," let us mention prudential regulators in charge of protecting dispersed and free-riding bank depositors and insur-

---

[13] To be sure, the financial contracts can be drawn entirely by the borrower. Still, in complex situations, it may be time- and resource-consuming to figure out the implications of certain types of covenants.

ees; and the delegated monitoring institutions associated with equityholders: lead investor (large shareholder, venture capitalist, leveraged buyout artist), board of directors, and capital market monitoring (proxy fights and takeovers).

• *Heterogeneity of claims.* Different securityholders have different interests simply because they have different claims on the firm. A well-known example is the antagonism between shareholders, who value revenue potential and some forms of risk-taking, and debtholders, who have more conservative incentives and care about the value of the collateral they will seize in case of default.[14]

The problem posed by the heterogeneity of claims has been tackled in a number of ways: covenants (as in the case of covenants limiting dividend distribution or debt accumulation by shareholders) combined with detailed disclosure of information about the firm's balance- and off-balance sheet activities; security design (for example, the protection of debt claims through convertibility options, collateral, and, in case of hard times, liquidation rights); legal framework (as in the case of the protection of minority shareholders); and institutions (such as the bankruptcy process) that organize renegotiation in distress.

Principle 7 (dealing with common agency): Corporate borrowing is plagued with common agency externalities. Various institutional responses, such as transparency, security design, and representation, have been introduced to deal effectively, although not perfectly, with the problems of contracting externalities, collective action and claim heterogeneity.

---

[14] Jensen–Meckling (1976).

Domestic liquidity provision

We will discuss later the need for an international lender of last resort (LOLR).[15] To follow this discussion, some background on the rationale for liquidity provision at the domestic level is required.

To have a reasonable chance to be able to meet their liquidity needs, firms and financial institutions can hold securities in other firms and financial institutions, to be sold on in a case of need. Liquidity created within the private sector is called *inside liquidity*. Intuition suggests, and formal analysis[16] confirms, that inside liquidity is sufficient for the private sector's needs[17] as long as

(a) the shocks faced by private sector entities are independent, and
(b) inside liquidity is properly allocated within the private sector.

In the absence of aggregate shock to the economy (condition (a)), good draws compensate for bad ones and no insurance needs to be supplied from outside the private sector provided that insurance opportunities are properly exploited (condition b). The latter requirement supports the pooling of liquidity at the level of financial intermediaries, since "autarkic" liquidity hoarding by

---

[15] The following material is drawn from chapter 4 of Holmström–Tirole (2001b) to which we refer for more detail.

[16] See Holmström–Tirole (1998). Important work by Caballero–Krishnamurthy (1999, 2001a,b), Diamond–Rajan (2001) and Kiyotaki–Moore (2000) studies situations in which liquidity may be insufficient even in the absence of macroeconomic shock because financing arrangements within the private sector waste liquidity.

[17] "Sufficiency" means that a safe store of value (e.g., a Treasury bond) that would be introduced in the economy would have no real effect and would command no liquidity premium (relative to standard asset pricing formulae. The reader is referred to Holmström–Tirole (2001a) for a general definition of liquidity premia).

each firm leaves lucky firms (those with no liquidity need) with excess liquidity[18] and thereby creates a waste of aggregate liquidity. Inside liquidity is sufficient in the absence of aggregate shock for the same reason that the risk of accident or fire can be mutualized through automobile or fire insurance.[19]

In the presence of aggregate shocks, however, the private sector must search for outside insurance. Outside insurance opportunities are created either by the existence of *domestic outside liquidity* provided by the State or by *foreign outside liquidity* supplied for the rest of the world.

This section focuses on the former type of outside liquidity, leaving the treatment of foreign outside liquidity for Chapter 6. But the following point is needed to affirm the relevance of domestic outside liquidity even for a country that has undergone full capital account liberalization and therefore has access to outside liquidity from abroad. (The arguments may appear to the reader at this stage a bit elliptic. They will be clarified in later chapters.) One might believe that, provided aggregate shocks are minor at the world level, a country's private sector can obtain all the liquidity it needs on the international financial markets. For example, Thai banks can purchase US Treasury bonds, the S&P500 index, or secure a credit line with a consortium of large international banks in order to insure against country-specific shocks. In fact, and as we will see, the scope for such foreign insurance is limited. Total foreign borrowing, which includes liquidity provision as one of its components, is limited by the country's international

[18] That they don't voluntarily redispatch to firms in distress because the latter do not offer a good enough financial return.

[19] The fact that the firms' idiosyncratic liquidity shocks may be endogenous (subject to moral hazard) does not alter this reasoning.

collateral. Buying US Treasury bonds requires borrowing abroad and crowds out borrowing destined to investment if foreign lenders expect to lose money in case of shock (i.e., if the securities are indeed used as an insurance device). The same point applies to international credit lines. Besides, it is not clear that a situation in which the foreign investors would fully insure a country against its macroeconomic shocks is desirable – international liquidity bails in foreign investors in adverse macroeconomic shocks, and therefore creates moral hazard for the government to the extent that it does not fully internalize the interests of foreign investors and is therefore more prone to eschew costly action that would make the occurrence of an adverse shock less likely.

We therefore support the bankers' and other financial market practitioners' conventional view that domestic outside liquidity matters. The source of domestic outside liquidity is the State. The State has a unique role in the provision of liquidity, for example[20] through the provision of deposit insurance with nonindexed premia, discount window facilities, indexed capital adequacy requirements, countercyclical monetary policy, a publicly funded social security system or implicit insurance of privately funded pension funds, unemployment insurance, and public debt management.

As always, an analysis of government intervention must begin with the key question: What can a government do that the private sector cannot, or is unwilling to, do? Our basic argument builds on the inability of consumers/investors to provide sufficient insurance direct to the private sector. The consumers' pledgeable income is

---

[20] See Holmström–Tirole (2001b) for a discussion of other ways in which the State provides liquidity to the economy.

quite small relative to their total income because they are not able to pledge their future human capital. This impossibility results from several factors: legal prohibition, transaction costs, possibility of moving abroad or hiding resources, and (for future generations) impossibility to contract. Whatever the reason, the fact is that consumers do not offer (unbacked) credit lines to corporations.[21]

In our view, the role of the State in the provision of aggregate liquidity (and more generally in economic life) stems from its *unique control rights*. These control rights include monopoly power on, inter alia, personal and corporate taxation, prudential regulation, monetary policy, antitrust enforcement, the legal system, labor market regulations, and central bank exchange rate policy.

While we will focus on the implications of the first control right, which underlies such liquidity determinants as the LOLR function, public deposit insurance, publicly funded unemployment insurance, a publicly funded social security system, and the provision of safe government securities, many other control rights held by the government affect aggregate liquidity.

Through the choice of capital adequacy requirements, liquidity ratios, and line of business restrictions, and through its enforcement policy, prudential banking regulators affect the sharing of risk between (in the absence of public deposit insurance) depositors or (under publicly provided deposit insurance) taxpayers on the one hand, and banks and thus more generally the corporate sector on the other hand. For example, the prospect of regulatory forbearance during crises reduces banks'

---

[21] Consumers do contract substantial future liabilities through mortgages. But a large fraction of these future liabilities is backed by the real estate collateral and therefore does not have the status of unsecured liabilitites.

demand for liquidity. So do deposit insurance premia that are not indexed on the banks' health: noncyclical deposit insurance premia provide banks with insurance against high interest rates and deposit contraction following negative banking shocks.

The legal system affects liquidity in several ways. A stronger corporate governance environment increases firms' pledgeable income, and, for a given level of investment, enables them to raise more money by issuing new securities in seasoned offerings. An efficient bankruptcy process has a similar effect. Of course, one ought to be cautious here, as the same factors also allow higher levels of investment and therefore increased liquidity needs. Labor market regulations affect the sharing of risk between workers and firms.

The State's ability to tax consumers implies that it can make some of the income of the current and future generations pledgeable. This implies that Ricardian equivalence – the neutrality of the State's fiscal/debt policy – does not hold; the State can help consumers and the corporate sector exploit their mutual insurance opportunities: *The corporate sector can hold explicit or implicit contingent claims on the government, which in turn holds explicit or implicit contingent claims on the consumers.* In other words, the State's unique ability to tax consumers makes it an intermediary in liquidity provision.

Outside liquidity is like an option: the corporate sector does not need it as long as everything goes well, and finds it very valuable when facing adverse macroeconomic shocks. Thus it seems natural to make at least some of the public liquidity provision state-contingent. While coupons on government bonds are usually not indexed on the health of the corporate sector, other public policies in practice create some state dependency of liquidity provision:

• Loose monetary policies that lower the interest rate in a recession raise the value of nonmatured bonds and thus the wealth of their owners. Traditional countercyclical monetary policies therefore have some flavor of state-contingent liquidity provision. We must recognize, though, that their effectiveness in this respect is bounded: monetary policy has its biggest impact on short term rates and a lower one on long term bond prices.

• Prudential forbearance, discount window facilities, and noncyclical public deposit insurance premia all go in the direction of providing state-contingent liquidity to banks.

• Procyclical social security contributions, public unemployment insurance, and similar measures provide state-contingent liquidity to firms.

Government bonds can improve economic efficiency by providing liquidity to the corporate sector. Namely, they build on the State's regalian power to tax personal income to make it possible for consumers to, indirectly and credibly, offer liquidity to the corporate sector.

It is tempting in this respect to view the disappearance of the equity premium puzzle in the US in the early 1990s as an (unintended) consequence of the large public deficits of the 1980s. The substantial increase in the stock of US Treasury bonds has reduced the liquidity premium commanded by bonds, and thereby brought the return on bonds closer to that on equities. [22]

---

[22] This possible argument for the decline of the equity premium seems to go the wrong way for the late 1990s. The decrease in government debt will reduce Treasury bills and bonds as a source of outside liquidity. On the other hand, what matters is the relationship between supply and demand for outside liquidity. With improved prospects, the demand for liquidity may also have shifted in the recent past. See, furthermore, the caveat on public debt as liquidity, stated overleaf.

While public debt may increase aggregate liquidity, it need not do so. All depends on the expected incidence of the corresponding tax burden. To understand this point, recall that the mechanics of liquidity provision through the issuance of Treasury bonds rests on a future transfer of wealth between consumers and the corporate sector. If, in contrast, economic agents anticipate that the bonds will be paid back through levies on the corporate sector, little liquidity creation is achieved. Outside liquidity is then created at the expense of corporate sector value and thus inside liquidity.[23]

---

[23] Unlike in the case of personal tax collection, tax authorities do not seem to have much intrinsic ability to raise pledgeable income in corporations beyond what can already be achieved by financiers.An increase in corporate tax to a large extent crowds out the income that can be pledged to investors.

5

Identification of Market Failure: Are Debtor Countries Ordinary Borrowers?

The proposals reviewed in Chapter 2 are direct transpositions of basic principles of capital adequacy, liquidity- and risk-management, and governance for corporations and financial institutions. Yet, while countries are often identified with corporate units with which they should share governance and financing principles, it is also frequently declared that countries have special features that somehow make them different. This chapter assesses these objections and then formulates the premises for my own perspective. I will argue that countries are indeed different, but the reasons I will emphasize differ from the usual ones.

The analogy and a few potential differences

Debtor countries are similar to ordinary borrowers in many respects. They lack the resources needed to finance high net present value (NPV) projects and must therefore borrow abroad. "Capital inflows" and "foreign investors" are the counterparts of "external funding" and "financiers" in corporate finance. As in the case of corporate financing, there is a wedge between the projects' NPV and the income that can be pledged to foreign investors. That is, investors may not be able to put their hands on all the proceeds attached to their investment.

Part of the reason is the same as for corporations: insiders enjoy private benefits and, further, must be given incentives to behave. But part of the reason is specific to the international context: investments financed by foreigners are used to produce both tradable and nontradable outputs, and because by definition foreigners have no demand for nontradables, the latter constitute an income that cannot be pledged to foreigners – a sort of "private benefit" automatically enjoyed by the host country. More precisely, while an individual borrower can always pledge some of its nontradable output to its foreign financiers, the latter must exchange this output against tradable goods (loosely speaking, the financiers must convert the domestic currency into dollars); this is where the aggregate constraint binds. There is in general a limited amount of uncommitted tradable resources held by domestic residents, to be exchanged against nontradable goods. A country's ability to borrow is therefore limited not only by its domestic borrowers' agency problem, but also by the extent of its "international collateral".[1]

Countries are also exposed to real shocks (the price of raw materials, the price of oil, competitive devaluations, recessions of key trading partners and so forth), just like ordinary corporations. This all suggests that a simple relabeling of variables permits the application of standard principles in corporate finance to international finance. So far, so good.

Some concerns have been voiced, however, against using this simple-minded analogy. Among them:

[1] To use an expression due to Caballero–Krishnamurthy (1999, 2001a,b).

- Governments can default on sovereign debt, or induce private sector default through a standstill, with much greater impunity than an ordinary borrower. The absence of an international bankruptcy court with extensive enforcement powers implies that countries lack some of the commitment available to ordinary borrowers. It is useful in this respect to remember the standard distinction between "ability to pay" and "willingness to pay". Domestic political constraints usually start biting before any technical capacity constraint (the physical ability to reimburse) is reached.[2]

For sure, a number of sanctions can be imposed by the international community against a country that defaults. As argued by Bulow and Rogoff (1988, 1989), defaulting countries may face financial sanctions, namely the freezing of financial and physical assets held abroad (for example, bank accounts may be frozen and aircrafts seized). Above all, they can face legal and trade sanctions, such as loss of the benefit of being able to avail oneself of international law.[3]

---

[2] Johnson (1997).

[3] "We believe that the primary motivation for repayment is the threat of direct sanctions that lenders can impose by going to creditor country courts and by influencing their domestic legislators. Such sanctions can cost defaulting debtor countries their ability to transact freely in the financial and goods markets. For example, if a country repudiates its foreign loans, it will be forced to conduct its trade in roundabout ways to avoid seizure. To compound this problem, the country will also be blocked from normal access to trade credits. Very short term trade credits, such as bankers' acceptances and letters of credit, are enormously important in reducing transactions costs in international trade. International banks can exploit economies of scale in monitoring costs to facilitate transactions between importers and exporters who sometimes know very little about one another.... Legal sanctions can also make consumption smoothing more difficult by preventing LDCs from openly holding assets in the industrialized countries for fear of seizure." (Bulow–Rogoff, 1989, p158–9)

Such sanctions strike two rocks. First, they affect different enforcers differently. For example, countries with strong trade or political links with the defaulting country may not want to give their assent to such sanctions. Furthermore, and unless a centralized organization, such as the World Trade Organization (WTO), succeeds in imposing sanctions on those countries that fail to punish the defaulting country, enforcement of the sanctions faces a familiar free-riding problem. Second, these sanctions are largely inefficient (rather than a pure transfer of wealth from the defaulting country to other countries). There is, therefore, a strong incentive to renegotiate them away after the country has defaulted. \in other words, even if the sanctions were enforceable, they may lack intertemporal credibility. This in part explains why we do not observe long punishment periods after a country has defaulted on its foreign debt.

• Investors cannot kick out management. Countries are sovereign and so foreign creditors cannot oust governments that have not defended their interests.

• There is no international lender of last resort (ILOLR) that could issue high-powered money.

Such arguments, while correct, seem irrelevant as they stand. As for the first two, and any other that would point at the fact that pledgeable income is low and incentives hard to set up in an international context, we should recall that in the corporate context there is a wide variety of borrowers. Some indeed have strong balance sheets. Others, such as high-tech start–ups, have weak balance sheets: no initial equity, no collateral, and no guaranteed income streams to pledge to investors. Furthermore, while the venture capitalist may be granted rights to kick out the entrepreneur, the latter may be so entrenched (or indispensable) that firing is not a realistic option. My purpose here is, of course, not to argue that countries are like start-ups. They aren't. Rather, the lesson to be taken from corporate finance is that "one size does not fit all", and that the same common premises give rise to a wide range of qualitatively similar – but quantitatively very different – financing arrangements. The fact that the contractual arrangements are highly context-specific does not negate the universality of the underlying principles. Put another way, the fact that countries are subject to limited sanctions should not in itself lead one to discard basic conclusions about financing arrangements.

As for the absence of a fully-fledged ILOLR, and as observed by Calvo (1998, 2000b), for example, LOLRs in advanced economies do not print money but rather issue debt to finance operations to rescue their financial systems. The relevance of the third argument therefore seems limited.

A dual-agency perspective

In my view, a key feature for the analysis of international borrowing relates to the nature and the exercise of control rights affecting the performance of private sector borrowers (firms or banks):

Dual-agency perspective:

1. Those control rights that are not vested with investors and affect the performance of the private sector borrower are actually shared between this nominal borrower and its government, giving rise to a dual-agency situation.

2. Investors contract with the borrower and not with the government.

3. Dual agency is much more relevant in a financially integrated economy than in a financially isolated economy, for two reasons:

- *The government has less incentive to defend investors' interests when those investors do not vote and, more generally, have limited political leverage.*
- *The government has a much greater degree of freedom in an open economy context as it can impact the tradable–nontradable mix.*

Governments nowadays hold much more extensive control rights and intervene much more in their countries' economies than they did during the previous period of high economic integration, namely before World War I. Before developing the argument in more detail, let's review how the many unique control rights held by the government in fiscal, monetary, exchange rate, taxation, and institutional infrastructure matters can impact the return of investors in general and that of foreign investors in particular.[4]

(a) Control rights affecting the exchange rate

Foreigners are ultimately reimbursed in tradables. Any government policy that reduces the amount of tradable goods that can be returned to foreigners[5] can exert a negative externality on foreign investors (foreign investors care about, say, dollars, rather than tradables per se. Here we are using "tradables" as a proxy for "dollars" and ignoring the fact that perfect correlation between the two is not perfect. Even when they hold domestic-currency-denominated assets, foreigners are

---

[4] The following list, although quite long, is not meant to be exhaustive.

[5] The work of Caballero–Krishnamurthy (1999, 2001a,b) very usefully illustrates the role of international collateral in crises. They emphasize themes rather different from those discussed here, as their models have no government moral hazard.

ultimately reimbursed in dollars, euros, or yen. The domestic claims held by foreigners can be traded at a decent exchange rate only if the country produces enough tradables).

Examples of government moral hazard with respect to the tradable-nontradable mix include:

- encouraging the channeling of investments to the nontradable sector, most commonly in real estate
- failing to sink export-promoting investments, for example investments in public infrastructure for tourism
- depleting international reserves, as when the government uses foreign reserves obtained in a sterilized intervention to boost domestic spending in tradables, or unsuccessfully defends a peg
- taxing exports
- failing to diversify exports, thus making repayment to foreigners riskier
- encouraging currency and maturity mismatches by the domestic private sector, again making repayment to foreigners riskier [6]
- encouraging a devaluation or depreciation of the currency (e.g., through the monetarization of deficits) when foreigners hold domestic-currency denominated assets, and
- engaging in forms of moral hazard highlighted in sovereign debt commentaries:[7] suspending convertibility, declaring a moratorium on sovereign debt, repudiating the debt, or nationalizing foreign assets.

---

[6] It may be objected that some less developed countries have no choice, as domestic-currency-denominated assets have "no market". But the absence of such a market is endogenous and highly related to the considerations presented here.

[7] Pioneered by Eaton–Gersovitz (1981) and Bulow–Rogoff (1989).

Thus, even leaving aside the direct forms of expropriation that are subject to sanctions (the last item on the list), there are many other and more subtle ways in which the government can impact the return earned by foreign investors. Certainly, most of these policies are likely to have other important macroeconomic consequences and may thereby inflict losses on some classes of domestic residents. The impact on domestic residents is factored in when selecting policies, but it does not affect our basic point (to be emphasized later in this chapter): when making trade-offs at the margin, a government is likely to underinternalize the value of foreigners' claims.

Indirect evidence concerning the political incentive to underinternalize foreigners' investments is provided precisely by countries' partial attempts at *committing* not to jeopardize foreigners' interests. In the past, a widespread commitment against excessive private sector borrowing consisted in the central bank's linking of borrowing in foreign currencies with the firms' forecasted exports. Some countries enact laws imposing limits on their fiscal deficit or public debt. Yet another strategy, which we will discuss later at length, is IMF membership, in the same way that the WTO is used as a commitment device in the area of trade policies.

Clearly, such commitment devices are highly imperfect. For example, commitments regarding fiscal deficits and public debt have little bite if local governments (e.g. regions) enjoy substantial fiscal and borrowing autonomy where these are concerned.[8] More importantly

---

[8] For example, Argentina or Brazil, with their high degree of fiscal decentralization, may for those reasons have a hard time to credibly commit to fiscal restraint. Dillinger and Webb (1999) argue that fiscal decentralization in Brazil underpinned the recent budgetary and financial crisis.

still, these numbers are highly subject to manipulation. A similar point applies to commitments on net reserves.[9]

(b) Control rights affecting investor returns generally

As in the case of a closed economy, several government policies affect the extent to which suppliers of funds can recoup their investment:

- institutional infrastructure: change in corporate governance and bankruptcy laws, and in the resources affected to their enforcement
- liquidity provision: creation and management of domestic liquidity (see Chapter 4), and
- changes in tax, labor, and environmental laws.

These policies a priori affect domestic and foreign investors indiscriminately. However, to the extent that a poor institutional infrastructure benefits (ex post, although not necessarily ex ante) domestic entrepreneurs and managers, and that decisions with regard to tax, labor, and environmental laws affect primarily domestic stakeholders, a bias in government decison-making may result.

To these control rights can be added those affecting public liabilities and, therefore, the likely exercise of government control rights in the future. To the extent that future hardships will make it more likely that the government will be tough on investors in general and on foreign investors in particular, current policies that induce future government liabilities *indirectly* reduce investors' return. Such policies include regulatory forbearance (lowering the effective capital adequacy requirements for distressed banks, allowing lending based on the collateral's current market value – rather

---

[9] Recent cases in point are Russia and Ukraine, where the net reserves turned out to be smaller than what the international community believed.

than the value this collateral would fetch in case of country crisis, negligent oversight of risk management practices) and fiscal deficits.

This large array of control rights implies that foreign investors confront *moral hazard in team*[10]. Moral hazard in team refers to situations in which a principal's payoff depends on the joint effort of two (or more) agents. Here, the eventual repayment of funds lent to a domestic borrower depends crucially on both the borrower's and the government's behaviors. Furthermore, this dual-agency problem is asymmetric. While the suppliers of funds structure cash flow rights, control rights, and the staging of investment so as to alleviate borrower moral hazard, they do not contract with the government. The latter's broad set of control rights and its incentives, to which we now turn, make the dual-agency perspective relevant.

The government's incentives

To go further, we must predict how the government will make use of the unique control rights described in the previous section. There is no single prediction in the matter as the situation, and in particular the politics, varies substantially across countries. However, this does not mean that government behavior cannot be predicted from first principles.

One possibility is that the government has financial interests in, or more generally is captured (through friendship, bribes, or fear of a coup) by, the private sector, as in the crony capitalism story. For example, in many developing economies, much of the corporate assets are owned or controlled by a few families with

---

[10] Holmström (1982).

strong ties to the political power; well-known illustrations include the former Suharto regime in Indonesia and the Marcos regime in the Philippines.[11]

The possibility that the government's incentives could be aligned with the domestic borrowers' interests has the merit of great analytical simplicity, in that the government exercises its control rights in the way the borrowers themselves (ex post) would have exercised them. So the framework is analytically similar to the standard single-borrower framework, except for the crucial difference that individual lenders are unable to contract on covenants and the contingent allocation of control rights with the government.[12]

Alternatively, the government may be subject (or close) to an election and want to pander to the electorate.[13] This situation need not be inconsistent with the

[11] In their study of 3,000 publicly traded companies in nine East Asian countries, Claessens et al (2000) offer a fascinating description of corporate ownership in Asia. In most countries (Japan is one exception), a few families control a sizeable fraction of corporate assets and GDP. As is the case in a number of European countries as well, individuals can control corporations with a limited amount of shares thanks to dual-class shares (shares do not all carry the same voting rights), cross-shareholdings (companies own shares of each other) and pyramid structures. Claessens et al find that more than two-thirds of East Asian corporations are controlled by a single shareholder; that the top fifteen families control between 50 and 70 percent of corporate assets in countries such as Thailand, the Philippines and Indonesia, and 76 percent and 84 percent of GDP respectively in Malaysia and Hong Kong; and that older companies in these countries have more concentrated ownership.

[12] The situation is then similar to that of an agent faced with a time-inconsistency problem, in that it would ex ante like to commit to an ex post behavior that it won't abide by; that is, the ex post incentives are ex ante detrimental. Note also that the government, in this scenario, may not fully internalize the losses incurred by third parties, such as the domestic taxpayers in the crony capitalism theory. In this case, an externality problem (as in Jeanne–Zettelmeyer 2000) is added to the time-inconsistency one just mentioned.

[13] See Maskin–Tirole (2001) for a description of the incentives for pandering and its implications for political design.

first, as the government may want to favor the industry in those decisions that pit it against foreign investors' interests. The pandering hypothesis, though, allows for a richer set of government behaviors, as when the government favors other domestic constituencies.

The basic requirement for this theory is for the government to have an incentive to favor domestic interests over those of foreign investors. We can allow a government to somewhat internalize the welfare of foreign investors through its concern about maintaining access to international markets, as long as this reputation mechanism is not sufficiently strong to eliminate all forms of moral hazard vis à vis foreign investors.

Discussion

Let us pause for a moment and discuss the relevance of the previous considerations about a government's control rights and incentives.

(a) But isn't this just the same in a closed economy?

Doesn't the US government impact the return of investors in General Motors, Intel, or the Silicon Valley start-up? The answer is that it does, but that the dual-agency problem is much less relevant in a closed economy context, for the two reasons stated above. Investors are domestic investors and so the incentive to bias decisions against them is obviously smaller. Foreigners do not vote and have only limited political leverage. And there are many fewer ways in which the return to investors can be reduced because government actions do not impact the exchange rate.

It may be the case that, while not being able to affect the value of its currency relative to that of the rest of the United States, the state of Texas, say, can still impact the price of tradables relative to nontradables, for example by encouraging investments in real estate or other products that are primarily consumed locally rather than in the rest of the US. But the set of instruments available to play such games is rather limited.

(b) Relationship to the fundamental view

The fundamental view discussed in Chapter 2 mostly emphasizes the role of implicit government guarantees to financial intermediaries in generating crises. As in the fundamental view, the focus here is on the government's discretion, although on a wider range of discretionary behaviors. The fundamental view focuses on issues which are primarily domestic in that the victims of the government's policies are the domestic taxpayers and workers affected by the ensuing recession. In a sense, the fundamental view depicts one polar case in which the government exerts no negative externalities on foreigners.[14] In contrast, here we analyze (potential) externalities on foreign investors. The policy implications accordingly are sharply different.

(c) How important is moral hazard?

Some economists downplay the role of government moral hazard. For example, De Gregorio et al (1999, p45) argue that

> There is little evidence that government moral hazard is widely present. The record is that following a crisis most governments lose power – not just in democratic countries and they all know it. The crisis itself is a blow to their claim to economic competence. It often hurts some

---

[14] As discussed in Chapter 2, there is a different fundamental view in which the borrowing country and its foreign investors engage in the "moral hazard play" and try to draw the IMF and the creditor countries' governments into contributing to rescheduling agreements. This play, if successful, obviously exerts negative externality on foreigners.

of the private interests that may have been crucial to their lease on power. And the IMF programmes that follow further erode their power.

There is clearly a grain of truth in this assertion. Yet one should refrain from jumping to the conclusion that government moral hazard is not central to the international financial infrastructure, and this for two reasons.

First, the fact that a manager may lose his or her job when the firm is in distress does not prevent managers from misbehaving. The threat of losing one's job certainly provides a countervailing incentive, but it is not in itself sufficient to prevent misbehavior. Other incentives and governance features must complement this threat in order to provide the manager with proper incentives. Similarly, the government – all else being equal – would like foreigners to be repaid, but when there is a political cost to reducing the probability of nonrepayment, the government may not fully internalize the foreigners' claims and may at the margin take insufficient precautions.

Furthermore, the threat of losing one's job may in certain circumstances *increase* moral hazard. In particular, a manager of mediocre performance has an incentive to take undue risk ("gamble for resurrection"). And there is nothing specific to the corporate context here: the same incentives apply to politicians facing reelection, for instance.

Second, and importantly, "government moral hazard" is given a narrow definition by most commentators. It refers to the investors' expectation of a bailout by the government (possibly with the help of official creditors), that is (a subset of) the second type of forms of government moral hazard listed above. Actions that directly impact the value of foreign investors' assets (in particular, in the exercise of those control rights affecting the tradable–nontradable mix) are less likely to generate a political backlash.

(d) Can sovereign rights be relinquished?

We have seen that corporate borrowers facilitate their financing by accepting to relinquish some of their control in a case of poor performance. Can the same idea be applied to governments to the extent that their actions impact the foreign investors' returns? It is a fact that sovereign states cannot surrender control rights as easily as corporations. Yet sovereign states do surrender control rights in practice. IMF membership does impose constraints. And, even though they are not always fully enforced, the many items on the conditionality list of rescue packages (see Chapter 1), coupled with the widespread feeling that IMF conditions are arduous, demonstrate that further encroachments on sovereignty are accepted in case of distress.

Thus sovereignty does not negate the general principles. It just limits the set of conditions that can be imposed. But again this observation is not specific to countries (even though it matters even more than in the case of corporations). Creditors of a firm in distress would be unable to enforce compliance to a rescue package demanding that workers work a stressful, fifty-hour week or that management disclose information that would hurt its interests. In the international financing context, the implication is that the impact of the surrendered rights on the country should not be so negative that the government prefers to sacrifice the country's reputation and face sanctions[15] than abide by its promises. The principle of

---

[15] Such as denial of access to the next tranches of the rescue package, trade sanctions, or else the seizure of financial or trade-related assets.

comparing relative willingness to pay for control helps in this respect, since it focuses attention on those rights that least hurt the country for a given level of investor protection.

This point sheds light on a first link between ownership – the idea that the country should voluntarily sign up to the policies laid out in a rescue package – and conditionality. From an abstract point of view (agency theory), an agent will do a better job for the principal if his objectives are well-aligned with those of the principal.[16] In our particular context, and for those conditions whose actual realization (the *spirit* rather than the letter) hinges strongly on co-operation by the country, congruence is quite important. So conditions that require adherence by the country should involve some degree of ownership (ownership is not a goal here, but a necessity). We will discuss a second link in Chapter 6.

A common-agency perspective

Let us now introduce our second key ingredient: common agency; and begin our discussion of the common agency problem in the context of sovereign debt (it is equally relevant for private sector borrowing, as we shall see).

While the importance of private debt crises will continue to grow as the role of government decreases, "old-style" sovereign debt crises are still, and will continue to be, relevant. For example, the crises in Mexico, Russia, Brazil, and more recently Ecuador, Pakistan, Romania, and Ukraine were primarily sovereign debt crises.

---

[16] See De Bijl (1994).

Were the sovereign to borrow from a single lender, this lender and the government would contract to their mutual advantage, taking account, of course, of the agency considerations inherent in the borrowing relationship. While these agency considerations would seriously constrain the gains from trade between the two parties, and therefore the level and terms of the financing agreement, there would be no market failure. The resulting agreement would just be the best one that could be drawn between the two parties. In contrast, a situation in which the government borrows (simultaneously or sequentially) from multiple lenders, is ripe with potential market failures.

As we discussed in Chapter 4, the absence of a "grand contract" under which the government and all its lenders would sit at the same table and draw together the terms of their relationship, penalizes the debtor country. The noninternalized externalities imposed on the other lenders by the financing deal between a lender and the government induces inefficiencies that, in the context of a competitive capital market, are passed through by investors and are ultimately borne by the borrower (the country).

Transposing the discussion in Chapter 4 to sovereign borrowing, the common agency problem may lead to overborrowing. When a lender lends to an already over-indebted country, the lender and the government are fully aware that the loan will make it harder for the country to repay its debt. The lender, however, cares little about it as he demands the corresponding risk premium. The other lenders, though, see their claim devalued. Similarly, the common agency problem may affect the composition, and not simply the level, of borrowing. When tilting the loan maturity structure toward the short term, the individual lender and the government do not internalize the potential reduction in the value of other investors' long-term claims brought about by an increase in the probability that the country will be liquidity-constrained in the near or medium term.

The government and its foreign lenders ideally would co-ordinate – write a "grand contract" – in order to solve this contracting-externality problem. This requires listing the many ways in which the government may mortgage the future by borrowing abroad, directly or indirectly, creating a monitoring structure to verify the transparency of governmental reports, and imposing conditionality and sanctions in case of violation. Recalling the common agency discussion in Chapter 4, this is where the collective action problem comes in.[17] As in the case of corporate borrowers, the collective-action problem refers to the monitoring of the financial arrangement, to intervention in case of violation, and to renegotiation in case of distress. Investors individually have a very suboptimal incentive to commit the resources to accomplish these tasks, and free-riding is likely to ensue.

In all this, there is no conceptual difference from the situation where a firm borrows from multiple investors. The key issue then is whether responses similar to those conceived in the context of corporate borrowing can be devised for sovereign debt. We will address this question in the next two chapters.

---

[17] For conciseness, we leave aside the issue of claim heterogeneity. Sovereign debt claims are heterogenous, for example, to the extent that they have different maturities or are secured (say by oil revenues) or not. Also, different official or even private lenders are affected differently by sovereign default. Heterogeneity is even more pronounced when one adds private sector borrowing: The interests of investors in FDI and short-term debt and of official and private claimholders are certainly not aligned.

We conclude this section by stressing the relevance of the common-agency problem for private sector borrowing as well. Recall the dual-agency perspective: foreign investors can design contracts with private borrowers that properly reflect the divergence of objectives between them; what they cannot do is contract with the government despite the fact that the latter's exercise of unique control rights affects their returns. As we will discuss at length in Chapter 6, this situation gives rise to contracting externalities and collective-action problems. Individual investor-borrower pairs take no account of the impact of their lending arrangement on the government's incentives and therefore on the returns of other private sector deals. And, to the extent that government moral hazard can be alleviated through policy commitments, monitoring of these commitments, and sanctions in case of violation, private lending is subject to the same free-riding concern as sovereign lending. For this reason, we will apply our "representation hypothesis" in Chapter 6 to private and sovereign borrowing alike.

6

Implications of the Dual- and Common-Agency Perspectives

This chapter derives the implications of the market failure identified in Chapter 5. Government moral hazard limits a country's access to financing. The country's government is an agent common to all foreign investors in both sovereign and, owing to the dual-agency structure, private sector borrowing. The country's access to more and better forms of financing is enhanced if the common-agency problem is alleviated through the introduction of a "delegated monitor"; and if public policies address the market failure rather than the symptoms. Lastly, the need for a delegated monitor and the nature of the policies differ across countries according to some identifiable patterns. The implications for the international financial architecture will be drawn in Chapter 7.

Implication 1: the representation hypothesis

(a) The broad picture
We can now conduct a thought experiment and look at the deal that the country (domestic private sector and government together) would like to strike with foreign investors at the capital inflow stage, if they could indeed contract. To perform this thought experiment, it is useful to turn to the analog of the simplified corporate finance

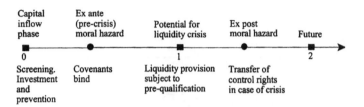

Figure 7.

framework of Chapter 4, adapted to the international context in Figure 7.

To enable both it and its private sector to have access to attractive levels and forms of financing, the government would like to reduce the extent of its moral hazard vis-à-vis foreign capital. Following the principles enunciated in chapters 4 and 5, this means:

- committing to and facilitating the transparency of country (sovereign and private sector) indebtedness and risk exposure through systematic disclosure of information, in the same way that corporate borrowers accept to enhance the readability of their on- and off-balance sheet positions and commit to limit their borrowing and manage their risks
- designing policies (or "covenants") that will prevent the government from, or reduce its incentive for, lowering the value of the foreign investors' claims. The choice of these covenants should obey the "relative willingness to pay principle" (principle 3). That is, they should be ranked by the ratio of their investment protection efficacy over the cost to the country; and
- accepting the principle of conditionality, where the extra control rights transferred to creditors in a case of poor performance obey the same logic as the initial covenants.

(b) The representation hypothesis

Implementation of the commitments just alluded to – limits on borrowing, transparency, policies reducing the misalignment of the government's incentives with investor interests, conditionality – needs to address the common-agency problem. The credibility of the commitments hinges on the presence of a "delegated monitor".

In this respect, an interesting analogy can be drawn with banking regulation. Most bank debt is held by small creditors. In the view of many private and central bankers, regulation is motivated, in particular, by the need to protect these small depositors who are, by and large, unsophisticated, in that they are unable to understand the intricacies of the balance-sheet and off-balance sheet activities of their banks, and (more importantly for our purpose, since international investors are rather sophisticated) are free-riders, who don't monitor their banks. Therefore, there is a *potential* market failure, in that a public good – the monitoring of the bank by its creditors – has to be supplied. But because individual depositors don't have an incentive to monitor the bank, someone has to do that for them. In work with Mathias Dewatripont (1994a), I argued that the banking regulator, through various activities, should represent the depositors. These activities take place ex ante – seeing to it that the bank meets capital adequacy requirements to ensure that there is enough equity within the bank to protect the depositors, and making sure that the bank is doing the right thing in terms of risk management – and ex post – in case of a crisis, intervening by closing or restructuring the bank, or forcing divestiture of some assets and imposing a line of business restrictions.

The analogy does not stop with the representation hypothesis, however. A key factor in a satisfactory fulfillment of the mission is reputation-building by both types of supervisors (international financial and banking). While identification of the market failure pins down the agency's mission *at the conceptual level*, it still leaves much discretion in the implementation of the mission. Just as, and probably even more so than, for banking supervision, the devil is in the detail when overseeing country-level borrowing. Assessing whether a country is "undercapitalized" or has too much "value at risk" is a highly technical matter, that does not yet admit satisfactory codification. And while the recommendation to "select conditions that defend investor interests at the lowest cost to the country" is straightforward, drawing a list of such conditions in practice is no easy task. The international financial agency must ex post strike a delicate balance to protect foreign interests without inflicting too much harm on the country. Finally, reputation is also key for the credibility of the pre-qualification mechanism and that of the ex post programmes.[1] The agency's ability to build and maintain a reputation is facilitated by the existence of a clear mission and, as we will argue in Chapter 7, by some degree of independence from political pressures, but it is by no means a foregone conclusion.

(c) Ownership and conditionality

The analysis sheds light on the current debate between ownership on the one hand – the idea that the country should voluntarily sign up to the policies laid out in the rescue package, supported for instance by the current

---

[1] This credibility might be enhanced by the adoption of graduated programs in the tradition of banking regulation. For example, the Federal Deposit Insurance Corporation Improvement Act (FDICIA), voted in the US in 1991, defines five levels of capitalization corresponding to five different levels of intervention/surrendering of control rights by the bank.

IMPLICATIONS 101

IMF managing director, Horst Köhler,[2] and (among those who argue against conditionality) the Meltzer commission and Jeff Sachs – and the traditional conditionality approach on the other hand. At any given point of time, conditionality and program ownership seem incompatible, merely by definition: there is no need to force someone to do what they would have done anyway. Yet conditionality and ownership can be reconciled by separating them temporarily. As the analysis shows, *ex post* (Stage 1) *conditionality* and ex ante (Stage 0) pre-qualification are perfectly consistent with *ex ante ownership*.

To illustrate this point, it is useful to return to principles 2 and 4 of Chapter 4, and illustrate them in the case of a firm or bank borrower. In this case, the prequalification takes the form of proper risk management, lines of business restrictions, and leverage ratios or capital adequacy requirements. A further set of measures comes into play if the firm or bank starts getting into trouble, that is ex post. These measures, for example, call for the banking regulator to intervene in and impose conditions on the bank. The conditions serve two purposes: they act as a disciplining device, and thereby tend to discourage the bank from getting into trouble; and they restrain the bank's ability to gamble for resurrection by taking a lot of risks when it is in trouble. Similarly, when a firm borrows – either from a bank or from bondholders – it signs off on a set of covenants that

---

[2] On April 29, 2001, the IMF's International Monetary and Financial Committee issued a communiqué endorsing "streamlined conditionality". It wants to focus on conditions related to macroeconomic objectives and give debtor countries a chance to build political support for the reforms. The scope of conditionality is the object of a heated debate, even within the International Monetary Fund. The reader will find a very readable discussion of ownership and conditionality in Kahn–Sharma (2001).

transfer control rights to those debtholders in case of poor performance – e.g., the nonrepayment of short-term debt. The borrower *ex ante* benefits from and therefore is willing to sign up to these conditions – a situation akin to ownership.

Implication 2: policy analysis

As discussed in Chapter 2, there is widespread consensus that currency and maturity mismatches (as well as other related factors such as the low penetration of foreign investments in domestic banking) have a very detrimental impact on the countries and by all means should be avoided.

This consensus against dangerous forms of finance seems misguided as a wide-range principle. Short-term, foreign-currency-denominated borrowing is a *limitation on government moral hazard*. Suppose, for example, that the country's liabilities were denominated in the domestic currency. Then, the government would have an incentive to consume (or induce domestic consumption of) tradables and to promote the production of nontradables, a strategy which in the end could leave foreign investors with an empty shell (since they don't value nontradables). Similarly, short-term debt allows foreigners to run for exits if the government starts misbehaving.

My main claim is that, as long as governments do not put equal weight on domestic and foreign interests, the efficiency of decentralized lending to a country must be evaluated in the light of its impact on government incentives. It bears emphasizing that *lenders and borrowers have no individual incentive to constrain government moral hazard*. A domestic company or bank and its lenders usually takes the macroeconomic forecasts as given, as they know that their financing arrangement will have a negligible impact on government behavior. So there is no reason why the market solution corresponds to the co-ordinated outcome: there are contracting externalities.

Put another way, the previous warning against drawing hasty conclusions regarding dangerous forms of debt only *suggests* why these conclusions might be unfounded. This warning is based on a collective incentive reasoning. The divergence between individual and collective incentives, though, calls for further analysis, which we now turn to:

• *Liability denomination*

To provide a first illustration of contracting externalities, consider the foreign investors' choice at the margin between investing in the tradable goods sector and investing in the nontradable goods sector. "Investing in the nontradable goods sector" must be understood in a broad sense as the acquisition of claims whose value is linked to the nontradable–tradable goods exchange rate (proxied by the exchange rate). Thus it includes not only lending to nontradable goods manufacturers and foreign direct investment in telecommunications and energy utilities, but also lending to banks or conglomerates with substantial investments in nontradables (including domestic real estate) and taking collateral in nontradable goods (such as commercial real estate). This last point is a bit subtle and requires some elaboration. A foreign creditor's formally dollar-denominated debt that is secured by real estate in a sense is partly domestic-currency denominated, as the borrower's default transfers to foreign investors a claim whose value to them is highly sensitive to the exchange rate.

The combination of government moral hazard and common agency implies that, contrary to conventional wisdom, the market outcome may involve foreign investors' claims that are excessively labelled in domestic currency (in the broad sense just defined). To see this, note that the foreign investors' value at stake in the case of depreciation of the currency is higher when the marginal investment is in domestic rather than in foreign currency. Therefore, if the foreign investors' overall interest lies in a strong domestic currency, the market underincentivizes the government to take precautions that decrease the likelihood of a depreciation of the currency. Adopting policies – or forcing the country to adopt policies – that encourage borrowing in domestic currency only aggravates moral hazard in this environment.

Interestingly, the extent and direction of the bias and of government moral hazard depend on the country's intertemporal mix of tradable and nontradable inputs and outputs. The same fundamentals imply that, *in other circumstances*, foreign investors may be hurt by an appreciation rather than by a depreciation of the currency. Consider a domestic export-producing firm that borrows abroad to buy machinery and equipment and whose only other input subsequently is local labor (think of a pulp paper manufacturer in Finland). Depreciation of the currency reduces the price of this labor relative to the international output and thereby benefits foreign investors. Government moral hazard in a country populated by such firms takes the form of an over-appreciation of the currency. And the common-agency problem implies that an increase in foreigners' holding of domestic-currency-denominated assets mitigates government moral hazard.

• *Liability maturity*

Applying similar reasoning to debt maturity, one can see that the market solution may be (although it need not be) biased toward *long* maturities. Suppose for simplicity that domestic firms borrow in foreign currency; that they must repay short-term debt using domestic net revenue as well as export revenue; and that this domestic net revenue is positive. Short-term debt is costly to individual borrowers, who run the risk of lacking liquidity at the intermediate stage. So in general they will choose a mix of short-term and long-term debt. Suppose now that all domestic firms tilt the mix at the margin, with a bit more of short-term debt and a bit less of long-term debt. The domestic firms then become a bit more vulnerable to exchange rate depreciation because the latter reduces the value of their domestic net revenues and thereby drains their liquidity. A government that puts substantial weight on the welfare of domestic firms will therefore think twice before adopting policies, such as the depletion of foreign reserves, that are likely to lead to a depreciation of the currency.

The fundamental point to be stressed, thus, is that without further analysis, there is no theoretical presumption that foreign investments are biased in favor of debt over equity, in favor of short-term debt over long-term debt, or in favor of dollar-denominated debt over domestic currency-denominated debt. A public policy that tinkers with the structure of private financing arrangements needs to consider its impact on government behavior.

Furthermore, the arguments above should not be misconstrued as opening the door to risky government policies. Indeed, country risk management that either

alleviates or does not affect government moral hazard is
desirable. For example, policies that would amount to
pure gambling on the central bank's international
reserves are not advisable.[3]

To illustrate this, consider the case of a government-
owned raw material producer whose international
market price is subject to a great deal of uncertainty. A
direct hedge against price fluctuations obtained in a
commodity derivatives market is a better insurance
device than sovereign borrowing in domestic currency.
The latter indeed provides insurance as the exchange rate
depreciates when the world price of the raw material
tumbles, implying lower debt repayments in foreign
currency. But it aggravates the government's moral
hazard problem because it makes currency depreciation
less costly to the country. Interestingly, Mexico has
issued oil-linked bonds.[4]

Exchange rate regime

Policymakers, academics, and public opinion have
devoted much attention to some spectacular currency

[3] For this reason, sterilized intervention may not be neutral even if all
markets (labor, goods, assets) are frictionless. [Asset market frictions create
scope for nonneutrality of sterilized interventions in Caballero–Krishnamurthy (2001b).] The exchange (in reduced form) of government assets for
foreign assets increases the amount of international reserves that the government can play with. It may thus induce the government to run fiscal deficits or,
more generally, to directly or indirectly consume international reserves.

[4] Along these lines, Brealey (1999) suggests the use by the government of
equity swaps with payments indexed on the level of the domestic equity index.
Such swaps would indeed provide useful insurance to the country, but unlike
bonds indexed on world raw-material prices they would aggravate government moral hazard, as foreigners would have a large stake in the domestic
stock market. Brealey suggests that the indexing could alternatively be based
on a regional equity index. Similarly, GDP-indexed bonds (such as those
issued by Bulgaria) may aggravate the moral hazard problem.

crises associated with pegged exchange rates. It would be illusory, though, to think that the underlying problem will disappear with the advent of flexible exchange rates. Misalignment of a government's and international community's preferences does not go away with a change in exchange rate regime. For this reason, the treatment above did not draw a distinction between, for example, "depreciation" (a fall in the currency's value) and "devaluation" (a resetting of the par value of a currency to a lower level).

The extent and implications of government moral hazard, though, do depend on the exchange rate regime. In the crises described in Chapter 1, pegs have proved very costly to the countries and have compounded their difficulties.

It is perhaps puzzling why, in spite of the wide intellectual consensus that pegged exchange rates are inadequate in a world of high capital mobility, countries have been so reluctant to abandon them. A look at government incentives offers a possible answer to this puzzle. Suppose that foreign investors are "depreciation averse" in that their assets in the country will be more valuable (in dollar terms) if the country's currency remains appreciated. Expectation of a strong currency accordingly benefits domestic borrowers, who can borrow more and under better terms. A government willing to help domestic borrowers then wants to convey signals to foreign investors that the country's currency will remain strong. One such signal is pegging of the currency.

A peg is costly as it jeopardizes the country's welfare should a crisis arise. The government may wastefully expend international reserves in an unsuccessful attempt to maintain the peg. But a government that is more likely to be able to maintain the peg also finds it relatively less costly to enter a peg than does a government which is likely to be less able to maintain it. This property underlies the use of a peg as a signal. As is usual in situations in which economic agents attempt to signal information through costly signals,[5] the result may be inefficient. There may be "excess pegging" – another form of government moral hazard.[6]

Cross-country comparisons

I argued that, as a general rule, the presence of a representative of foreign investors and careful policy design facilitate countries' access to higher levels and more attractive forms of financing. One would, however, not expect all countries to be the same in terms of their need for proper governance in the quest for foreign capital. The analysis above suggests that the magnitude of the problem hinges on the extent of government moral hazard.

The extent of government moral hazard in turn depends on

(i)   the "scale" of foreign borrowing
(ii) the range of control rights held by their government, and
(iii) the government's political incentives.

Regarding (i), note that scale is not all and that a better determinant of moral hazard is the stake foreigners have in the country. For example, foreign lending that is secured by oil revenues is not really at stake. Similarly,

---

[5] See e.g. Spence (1974), in the corporate finance context Ross (1977) and Myers–Majluf (1984) and, in the context of international finance, Jeanne (1999a,b).

[6] In the terminology of information economics, this particular form of moral hazard is called "adverse selection".

short-term claims are less at stake than long-term claims. We also observed that the foreign investors' stake in a government's policy hinges on the nature of the production technology (tradable vs nontradable inputs and outputs) and the currency denomination of their claims.

Regarding (ii), the range of control rights held by the government, countries in which the government has a lower degree of freedom should on average experience a lower demand for external commitment.

Finally, consider (iii). A government's political incentives are highly dependent on considerations of the political economy. I will make no attempt at providing a comprehensive overview of the impact of politics on the relevant incentives, but rather will content myself with illustrations of the ways in which politics may impact the moral hazard problem.[7]

Consider, for example, the cost of a policy that depletes international reserves to delay adjustments and boost domestic consumption. Let us posit that the resulting currency depreciation benefits domestic borrowers (say, their revenues are export revenues and their costs are in domestic labor), and that the workers/consumers are hurt by a depreciation (perhaps because the price of imported goods goes up). One would expect markedly different government policies depending on whom the immediate benefits of the policy can be channeled to and on whom the government is eager to please. A government captured by industry is likely to go for a weak currency, while one pandering to consumers would try to keep the currency appreciated. But one can easily envisage other situations in which the funda-

[7] Internal politics considerations have been much emphasized in trade theory (e.g., Bagwell–Staiger 2000, Grossman–Helpman 1994 and Maggi–Rodriguez-Clare 1998). In my view, they have received insufficient attention for capital-account matters.

mentals will induce different interest group preferences and therefore different political outcomes. Furthermore, which interest groups have political clout is country- and epoch-specific, as it depends for example on the current government's electoral concerns (or absence thereof).

Is there a need for an international lender of last resort?

Let us now turn to the issue of LOLR.[8] As discussed in Chapter 2, a number of economic experts have drawn an analogy between domestic liquidity crises and capital-account crises, arguing that international finance needs an ILOLR in the same way that countries have developed lending-of-last-resort services through the central bank and, more generally, the State.

To qualify this description, one should note that experts agree that large-scale external bailouts are not desirable. As is well understood, the cost of such bailouts is an implicit subsidy encouraging ex ante overborrowing by the country (or, equivalently, overlending by the foreign investors). (A separate issue with large bailouts is fundraising. It is well-known that it is hard to tax the global taxpayer without a world government. It might therefore be difficult to find the money needed to finance large bailouts, even if they were deemed to be desirable.)

---

[8] The standard definition of an LOLR (as given, say, by Bagehot 1873; see Chapter 7 of Freixas–Rochet 1997, Allen–Gale 1998, and Chapter 9 of Allen–Gale 2000b, for the modeling of the LOLR function), refers to the central bank's responsibility for accommodating demands for high-powered money in times of crises through open-market purchases or discount window loans at penalty interest rates to "solvent but illiquid" banks. See, e.g., De Bonis et al (1999), Giannini (1999, 2000), and Kenen (2001) for discussions of the LOLR function and its transposition to an international context. There is no World Central Bank, and so we define an LOLR as an institution that provides liquidity to a country when commercial lenders no longer want to supply funds.

This being said, we should realize that emergency lending by an ILOLR cannot by definition be completely safe. Many observers make a distinction between "illiquidity" and "insolvency". This distinction is unwarranted. There is never illiquidity without at least some suspicion regarding insolvency. If it were *known* that a country (or for that matter a corporation) in distress were solvent, then the country would immediately receive liquidity assistance from a private financier (or a consortium of private financiers).

My main point here is that the analogy with the domestic LOLR function is misleading. I argued in Chapter 4 that *domestic* liquidity is scarce and that the government therefore plays a key role in the provision of liquidity, one important aspect of which is the role of LOLR during a banking crisis. Issues are different at the international level. There is a priori no shortage of *international* liquidity. A Thai bank can buy US Treasury bonds, Euro-denominated bonds, or secure a credit line with large international banks. The limit is not their overall availability, but their availability to a country with limited international collateral (see Holmström–Tirole 2002).

Thus, the case for a LOLR is weaker than in the case of domestic liquidity since there is plenty of international liquidity around.

This does not necessarily mean that there is no case for a more limited LOLR function as a renegotiation enabling device. To put this into context, recall that the IMF has recently become a crisis manager by lending into arrears (but taking limited risks) and organizing the negotiations between the foreign investors and the government. The question of crisis management has two dimensions: positive (how to do it?) and normative (should we facilitate crisis resolution?).

Let us start with the positive question. As many have noted, the IMF is not strictly needed for this function. Commercial banks do concert in times of crisis; indeed, private co-ordination of bank creditors played an important role in the South Korean and Brazilian episodes. Bondholders are more numerous, but, as is the case for corporate borrowers, exchange offers and collective action clauses can then facilitate the rescheduling or write-down of the bonds. A case can be made, though, for the IMF as a natural crisis manager, to the extent that short-term support buys time for renegotiation and the conditionality that it will help enforce is part of the negotiation.

The normative question is not as straightforward as it seems. From the topsy-turvy principle (see Chapter 2), a more efficient crisis resolution reduces the cost to the government of entering into a crisis and therefore makes the crisis more likely. Indeed, the contract-theory literature has most often emphasized the detrimental effects of renegotiation. Theoretical arguments in favor of enabling renegotiation are that (a) in a common agency/unco-ordinated lending situation, renegotiation may have benefits[9] and (b) contracts may be somewhat incomplete, and renegotiation may help complete them. My gut feeling in the matter is that advocates of efficient crisis resolution are right in stressing ex post benefits over the ex ante cost. But this is ultimately an empirical matter.

---

[9] The theoretical literature on renegotiation under common agency includes Martimort (1999) and Olsen–Torsvik (1993, 1995).

7

Institutional Implications: What Role for the IMF?

This chapter discusses the two fundamental (and hotly debated) questions concerning the International Monetary Fund: its mission and its governance. As we will see, the two questions are not unrelated.

From market failure to mission design

The IMF's original mission, defined in Bretton Woods in 1944, was to support a system of "pegged-but-adjustable" exchange rates. At the time, tight restrictions on capital mobility brought balance-of-payments issues to the fore. The IMF accordingly, and for many years, emphasized oversight of fiscal and monetary policies. Its customers could well be developed countries (for example, Italy in 1964 and the United Kingdom in 1967). And limited capital mobility implied that the IMF played little role as a crisis manager.[1]

Today's environment is quite different from those days. Capital account imbalances often swamp current account considerations. Customers are medium- and

---

[1] In fact, Article VI of its Articles of Agreement prohibits the use by a member of the Fund's general resources to meet a large or sustained outflow of capital. To the extent that IMF funding facilitates renegotiation, this Article in theory (although not in practice) limits the role of the IMF as a crisis manager. See Giannini (2000) for more details.

low-income countries with large external borrowings. And the IMF is often drawn into the role of crisis manager. Somehow these evolutions must have changed the IMF's mission. But what is this mission?

I observed earlier that too many objectives are conferred on the agency within the policy debate on the role of the IMF. These objectives create a lack of focus; furthermore they are often conflicting. A multilateral institution, like any organization, should not be a jack of all trades and master of none. Regardless of the merit of the arguments presented in this book, the reader will agree that multidimensional criteria bode no good economics, and that a coherent analysis requires a clearly stated objective function, which itself must be based on a clear identification of a market failure.

To subject myself to my own discipline and at the risk (the certainty!) of being oversimplistic, let me offer some views on what the international community could be trying to achieve in the first place (leaving aside for the moment the very important objective of fighting poverty). Following Chapter 6, the dual- and common-agency perspectives suggest a natural way of refocusing the IMF. In the case of private sector borrowing, the dual-agency perspective builds on the observation that foreign investors contract with individual borrowers and not with their government, resulting in a market failure. The country's welfare would increase if the government were to contract with foreign investors in a co-ordinated manner. The same point applies to sovereign borrowing, for which the absence of unified contracting with the government calls for the introduction of a delegated monitor.

This suggests that the IMF's role is to substitute for the missing contracts between the sovereign and individual foreign investors and thereby to help the host country benefit fully from its capital account liberalization. Accordingly, the IMF should act as a delegated monitor and a trustee for foreign interests precisely to facilitate the country's favorable access to foreign borrowing. It is worth emphasizing that the interests of foreign capital are not those that count in the objective function from an ex ante viewpoint. After all, competitive capital markets will generate ex ante fair rates of return to investors regardless of the degree of financial instability. The concept of ex ante ownership means that the country's interest is put at the forefront.[2]

The concept of delegated monitoring underlies the (controversial) IMF approach in terms of pre-qualification and conditionality[3] (which still leaves open the practical issue of which ex ante covenants and ex post conditions can be implemented effectively, but this is another matter). In this approach, the IMF offers a monitoring service to its members, enabling them to have access to more and better sources of finance.[4] The position advocated here adds to the standard approach by pointing at the market failure that motivates the exis-

---

[2] As discussed in Chapter 6, this position is very similar to that Mathias Dewatripont and I adopted to provide an integrated treatment of prudential regulation. In Dewatripont–Tirole (1994a), we started from the simple hypothesis that depositors (rationally) free-ride in the monitoring of their bank and need to be represented. This organizing principle leads to the view that supervisory authorities should have a biased mission, namely the defense of depositors (or the deposit insurance fund), rather than a broad and less well-focused objective of welfare maximization.

[3] The commitment aspect is also emphasized, e.g. in Sachs (1989), Claessens–Diwan (1990) and Rodrik (1996). As we have seen, while ex post conditionality is a long standing IMF policy, ex ante conditionality (pre-qualification) is still mostly an idea, since the CCL – the facility based on pre-qualification – has not been used to date.

[4] This service is not performed by the providers of private credit lines to sovereigns (as in Argentina, Mexico, and South Africa). Such credit lines do not involve a delegated monitoring function.

tence of the international financial institutions. This identification of the market failure allows us to analyze the institution's mission and policy responses within the same, unified framework.

Needless to say, the refocusing of the IMF as an official (as opposed to a de facto) advocate for rigor should not be detrimental to the poor.[5] It is therefore important that its anti-poverty programs[6] be taken up elsewhere, say by the World Bank (which would also gain in focus in the process). The fight against poverty is fundamental, and should be stepped up, but it does not seem to be a natural IMF mission. As the IMF has long realized, poverty reduction cannot be an object of conditionality.

The rest of the chapter discusses the governance of a multilateral organization entrusted with a delegated monitoring function.

Governance

The other hotly debated question concerning the IMF is its governance. The IMF historically has enjoyed a nonnegligible amount of autonomy despite a very high level of political accountability at a formal level. Indeed, IMF governance in theory bears little resemblance to

[5] There are actually cases (crony capitalism) in which discipline and the fight against poverty go together. Preventing the government from exercising forbearance vis-à-vis its rich friends and from shifting the burden to the rest of the economy (as in Asia) does not sound like a bad idea both from the narrow point of view of investor protection (the government may be less willing to support cronies if it knows it won't be able to help them in case of distress) and from the point of view of protecting less favored classes of the society.

[6] The IMF has been criticized for trying to be another development bank through programs, such as the Poverty Reduction and Growth Facility, that provide long-term loans at low interest rates to poor countries. While this criticism is sometimes a disguised attempt at cutting a form of aid to the poor that is not used for geopolitical reasons, the most serious critics view the issue as one of the optimal allocation of tasks among international agencies.

that of a central bank. Its oversight structure is highly political. The final authority rests with its Board of Governors, composed of 182 finance ministers or heads of central banks. Because governance by such a board is rather impractical, an Interim Committee (renamed "International Financial and Monetary Committee" in 1999), composed of the finance ministers from twenty-four countries, provides further oversight. The "day-to-day" management is delegated to the Executive Board, composed of twenty-four Executive Directors, who meet three times a week (more in case of a crisis). The Executive Directors sitting on that board are answerable to the governments. In practice, the permanent staff has a substantial say in the decisions. That is, it has substantial "real control" despite almost no "formal control".

There is a growing feeling both in academic circles (a notable and interesting exception is De Gregorio et al, 1999) and especially among popular opinion that the IMF is insufficiently accountable.[7] To address the question of optimal IMF accountability, let us return to some organizing principles.

Decision-making in cooperative undertakings

Any organization is run on a day-to-day basis by its full-time management and controlled by its overseers. In the context of an organization specialized in international finance, the multilateral organization is bound to have a highly heterogenous board. Governments are unlikely to agree on policies. This is most readily seen in the area of development aid. Donors' aid, with the exception of

---

[7] This trend is certainly not confined to the IMF. A similar complaint has been heard, for example, regarding the lack of democratic accountability of the WTO.

that from Nordic countries, has in the past been much
tainted by commercial, political, and military considerations and, except in its discourse, has not necessarily put
the humanitarian objective to the forefront. The same
problems emerge in the context of financial stability.
The United States government has been reported as
having put pressure on the IMF to agree to continue
financing Russia before the 1998 crisis even though the
country was not complying with previous conditions.[8]
More generally, regional, cultural, strategic, or trade
considerations imply that a group of powerful countries
within the organization have an incentive to lobby for
lenient policies when a country fails to abide by its
promises. Conversely, powerful countries with no such
vested interests but with high financial stakes in the crisis
country may lobby for excessively harsh conditions.

   Much recent research in economics has emphasized
the difficulty of managing organizations on behalf of a
highly heterogenous constituency. Conflicts of interest
among the board generate endless haggling, vote-trading
and logrolling. They also focus managerial attention on
the delicate search for compromises that are acceptable
to everyone; managers thereby lose a clear sense of
mission and become political virtuosos. The difficulties
encountered by organizations with a highly heterogenous membership are, for instance, well-documented
by Hansmann in his 1996 study of co-operatives. Hansmann makes a coherent empirical case for the benefits of
membership homogeneity. He shows that successful co-
operatives tend to be ones built around a simple objec-

---

[8] The United States is in a particularly strong position to influence IMF
policies because of its 17.56 percent share of votes. Because a number of
IMF decisions require an 85 percent majority, the United States de facto has
a veto right on these decisions and some leverage over other decisions (requir-
ing a 70 percent majority).

tive shared by its membership. Multilaterals, unfortunately, cannot afford this luxury. At best, they can be given a clear mission on which the members agree as a matter of principle, even though they have conflicting incentives when applying the broad principle to a specific country.

Economics of accountability

Even if all government delegates agreed on the proper role of the multilateral, there would still exist a problem that surfaces in all democratic institutions: representatives are accountable to voters and therefore have an incentive to be liked by them. They want to signal that they stand for the voters' interests, that their preferences are congruent. This often implies that politicians think *with* the voters instead of *for* the voters. In a nutshell, they pander to public opinion.

There can be no doubt that accountability is a good thing per se. It is important that officials are to some extent responsive to the electorate's wishes and do not pursue which are purely in their self-interest. However, the foundations of representative democracy, as embodied for example in the principles laid out during the American and French revolutions, are the need to delegate some of the decision-making to representatives who have more time and incentive to acquire decision-relevant information than do individual voters, and to prevent these representatives from obeying instructions given by their electorate. The purpose is defeated though, when elected officials cater to the electorate's prejudices so as to enhance the likelihood of their reelection.

In the context of a multilateral organization, the real danger is that the representatives of member countries put more weight on the impact of their stance on domestic opinion at home than on the objectives of the organization they are meant to govern. This problem is aggravated by the fact that a country's representative's expressed opinion or vote may have a minor impact on the final decision but a substantial impact on their reputation back home.

One way to reduce the incentive to use multilateral decision-making as a signal to the domestic electorate is to confine decision-making behind closed doors and not tolerate leakages to the press (not an easy task, by any means). This in a sense gives country representatives some independence and may help them internalize the mission of the organization. This approach is to some extent followed by the IMF's Executive Board. The twenty-four Executive Directors (who, remember, are answerable to their government or group of countries) usually decide by consensus and rarely record their votes or dissenting opinions. *Given the current governance structure*, this lack of transparency is, in my view, probably wise. It insulates the Executive Directors from the need always to signal to their governments and domestic public opinion, and thereby makes them more likely to identify with the organizational goals.

This of course does not imply that I favor a lack of transparency as a general rule. Indeed, more transparency would be highly desirable in a context in which Executive Directors were more independent. An independent Executive Director's incentive to please a political principal is much diminished. Transparency then has a beneficial impact on incentives, as it enhances legacy concerns.[9] Note that in this respect the disclosure of minutes, votes,

---

[9] For a formalization of the benefits of transparency for committees populated by independent members and its cost for committees composed of elected officials, see Maskin–Tirole (2001), from which the discussion in this section is more generally drawn.

and dissenting opinions that is practiced at the US Supreme Court and in some central banks (as in the case of the US, UK and Japan), occurs in institutions that are independent of the political power.

In many democracies there has been a broad shift of power toward independent officials, such as central banks, regulatory agencies, and judges. The benefit of decision-making by individuals who are shielded from electoral concerns is the much diminished incentive to pander. The cost of independence, of course, is that officials may get out of control and impose their own agenda on the people.

In this trade-off between political accountability and independence, independence is particularly valuable either when decisions are highly technical (the electorate has very poor self-knowledge and so its prejudices are likely to be incorrect) and their effect long delayed, or when majorities may oppress minorities. Intuitively, the cost of politicians' pandering to public opinion is high when this public opinion is likely to be misconceived[10] or when the majority's preferences are likely to diverge from social welfare.

Of particular interest for our purpose is the technicality of matters related to the financial system. There is no question that issues concerning international financial stability are highly complex and therefore unlikely to be properly grasped by non-specialists in the field. This casts some doubt on the effectiveness of political

---

[10] I do not associate this misconception with an intrinsic inability of voters to grasp the issues. Rather, my view is that we are all free-riders in the political realm. A voter individually has no impact on the political outcome and therefore rationally does not spend the hours, weeks, or years that would be necessary to thoroughly comprehend issues such as local loop unbundling, international financial crises or other such complex matters on which electoral candidates and platforms might be assessed.

accountability. On the other hand, one may be legitimately concerned about giving a blank check to technocrats in charge of overseeing the international financial system. In the end, some arm's-length political control is necessary. Political intervention should verify mainly that the institution fulfills its mission in the long term, but the political principal should not mingle in each and every decision. In such a world, technocrats are incentivized to fulfill their mission, both by concern for their legacy and by fear of dismissal once their mandate expires. This brings us to the point that agency missions that should be defined with reference to well-identified market failures, also have incentive consequences.

Before turning to the case for focus, let us stress that focus is not the panacea and that complementary incentives matter. For example, the presence of a highly professional staff (as has traditionally been the case at the IMF and WB, for example) is not only a source of legitimacy, but also one of incentives, to the extent that competent and specialized staffers tend to be more concerned about their intellectual legacy than others. Along similar lines, the presence of a respected and completely independent review board may help the agency acquire its sense of mission.

The benefits of focus

Besides being a response to a well-defined market failure, the mission here conferred upon the IMF carries the benefits attached to specialization. It is therefore worth reviewing the theoretical case for focus. To be honest, there is still limited knowledge in economics and political science as to how to structure government agencies and to inculcate a sense of mission. But a few general ideas start to emerge:

• *Focus.* In his classic study of government bureaucra-
cies, Wilson (1989) argues compellingly that the most
effective government agencies are those with a clear
sense of mission. Unlike for-profit companies whose
clear focus is on profit maximization, government agencies by their very nature are meant to promote the
internalization of various externalities and therefore
tend to have a long list of objectives; in a sense they
are the ultimate stakeholder society.[11] Wilson's case
studies point at the benefit that can be gained from
ignoring certain worthwhile goals to focus on a given
mission.

The theoretical analysis of multi-task career concerns
is broadly consistent with Wilson's view.[12] The performance of agencies such as the IMF will be reviewed by
political principals and by posterity. The agency officials'
concern for their legacy, their tenure in the job, or any
other incentive related to performance assessment makes
them particularly accountable if their performance is to
be benchmarked against a clear objective.

• *Conflicting tasks and division of labor.* The benefits
from focus are particularly high when the agency is
confronted with tasks that not only compete for its
resources but, further, conflict with each other. For
example, it is hard to ask a power utility to increase
electricity sales by providing a better service and lower
prices, and at the same time to reduce electricity sales
through demand-side management programs; or to ask
an attorney simultaneously to play the role of prosecu-
tor. Conflicting goals call for the creation of "advocates"
with biased objectives.[13]

---

[11] See Tirole (2001) for a discussion of incentives and governance in a
stakeholder-society context.
[12] See Dewatripont et al (1999a,b).
[13] See Dewatripont–Tirole (1999).

• *Carrot and stick.* While the previous two arguments were concerned with the agency's incentives, a different type of argument can be made regarding the beneficial impact of the monitor's focus on the monitoree's incentives. The regulation of economic agents may be facilitated by the conferring of contingent control rights to regulatory agencies with different incentives: namely, control rights should be given to a "soft" agency when performance is good and transferred to a "tough" one when performance falls below standard. In the same way that an ordinary corporation has to abide by conditions set by conservative creditors when it enters into arrears,[14] a public enterprise sees its effective control shift from a friendly "spending ministry" to the much less friendly finance ministry when its borrowing needs become serious. The threat of a big stick in case of arrears is clearly not without cost for the simple reason that distress may arise from bad luck and not solely from misbehavior.

The cost of focus

Focus is highly desirable and underlies the principle of separation of tasks among the international agencies, the so-called "WxOs" (where "W" stands for "world", "O" for "organization", and "x" for the issue to be addressed: health, environment, finance, development, etc.). Broadly speaking, the existing (IMF, WB, BIS, WHO, UN,WTO, ILO, et al) or to-be-created WxOs can be regrouped into three categories:

• "Externality-solving agencies" aim at preventing countries from exerting negative externalities onto

---

[14] See Dewatripont–Tirole (1994b, 1996).

each other: wars, environmental damage, trade restrictions, and so on.

• "Collective-action agencies" aim at coordinating richer countries' action toward less-favored ones in the realms of development, health, education, and so on. Their rationale is that the corresponding public good – to simplify, helping the poor – is supplied in insufficient quantity by bilateral donors (who attempt to free-ride on each other) and that the money allocated by these donors may be distributed inefficiently in accord with political considerations rather than humanitarian grounds.

• "Service providers" are international agencies that provide certification services to countries with respect to their labor, social, or banking practices, or their financial stability.

For example, the WTO is an externality-solving agency, the WB a collective-action agency, and the IMF a service provider (according to the argument set forth in this book). Unavoidably, though, the WxOs' tasks involve some overlap; for example, IMF policies impact the welfare of the poor in debtor countries. The by-product of the principle of specialization is the emergence of "cross-sectoral disputes". International agencies cannot avail themselves of arbitration services, in contrast with ministries within a government, which also reflect the principle of specialization but whose conflicts are settled by the prime minister.

To handle cross-sectoral disputes among WxOs, Jacquet et al (2000) suggest a three-step procedure (provided, of course, that time allows this process to take place – the scenario must be amended in a crisis-management situation): (1) an agency whose decision may adversely impact the fulfillment of another agency's mission asks the latter for an informed opinion; (2) the

decision-making agency either follows the other agency's opinion or motivates its decision not to follow it;
and (3) serious disputes are settled by a dispute resolution body. Steps (1) and (2) seem attractive. Letting
"advocates" express their views is likely to boost the
agencies' legacy concerns. Step (3) raises the tricky
issue of the dispute resolution body's mission and incentives, and may therefore require further elaboration.

Competition among agencies

An interesting question, which I will discuss only briefly,
is that of the scope for competition among several international financial agencies. The case for competition is
the standard one. If the IMF, say, does a poor job at
helping countries gain access to funds, or designs inefficient conditionality (i.e., imposes ex post conditions
where the cost to the debtor country is not commensurate with the benefit to the international community),
then countries will be able to turn to another agency
that will provide better certification or less costly crisis
resolution. To use an analogy (and with the obvious
caveat that the IMF's mission is quite different from
that of a rating agency), if Moody's and Standard and
Poors repeatedly do a poor job at rating the bonds issued
by corporations that hire them, the corporations will
turn to new rating agencies.

This being said, competition in this kind of activity
does not come about easily. Good knowledge of a country requires substantial investment and specialized staff,
neither of which is easily duplicated.[15] Competition
among agencies also entails a loss in "reputational

---

[15] Some evidence in this respect is supplied indirectly by the fact that large
private lenders, who do monitor the countries quite carefully, still make
substantial use of information collected by the IMF and the WB.

returns to scale". A key ingredient for an agency in successfully accomplishing its mission is, as we have seen, its reputation: reputation for monitoring carefully, for demanding investor-reassuring but fair-to-the-country conditions, and for enforcing these conditions. The smaller the number of countries that the agency interacts with, the more difficult it is to build a reputation. A third potential cost of competition among financial stability agencies arises when a country's crisis has considerable systemic consequences. Unless the countries affected by the spillovers are monitored by the same agency as the crisis country, cross-agency externalities may result.

Private solutions

Another interesting question, which I also won't expand on in the interests of brevity, is whether the delegated monitoring function could not be fulfilled by a grouping of private and official lenders.

While such "private solutions" may have been crowded out by the existence of the IMF, the available empirical evidence and theoretical insights are not encouraging either. Groupings such as the Paris and London clubs focus on renegotiation (of sovereign debt to official creditors and to commercial banks, respectively), and are insufficiently involved in the other activities of pre-qualification, monitoring, and conditionality that are part of a proper governance activity. In one case,[16] Peru in 1976, private creditors attempted to manage conditionality after the Peruvian government asked a consortium of six large US banks for a balance of payments loan without an IMF agreement in place, and accepted conditions and the banks' monitoring of

---

[16] Discussed in Rodrik (1996) and Stallings (1979).

these conditions. The experience proved a failure. Conditions were not met, and bankers, apparently fearing controversy and bad publicity, felt rather uneasy about policing the government.

Perhaps we should not be surprised by the apparent inability of private lenders, or of bilateral official lenders for that matter, to interact credibly with governments to offer them access to commitment. Private lenders don't quite seem to have the standing for the activity; neither do official lenders, whose incentives are often garbled by trade, cultural, or military considerations. And for the most part they are highly heterogenous: a proper grouping of private lenders would mix equityholders and debtholders, holders of short- and long-term debt claims, and holders of sovereign and private sector claims. Interests would therefore be somewhat dissonant. Efficient and expedient decision-making is unlikely to come out of such a gathering.

8

Conclusion

To conclude, let me review the book's argument:

- The lack of a clear mission for the IMF, and the current focus on symptoms rather than disorders, both suggest that we should return to identifying the underlying market failure.
- The market failure emphasized in this book stems from the absence of contracting with the government, notwithstanding the fact that the latter has many subtle and not-so-subtle ways of affecting the return to foreign investors.
- In order for the country to have access to more and better financing, foreign investors need to be represented. The IMF could therefore act as a delegated monitor, rebalancing the dual- and common-agency problems to the benefit of the borrowing country.
- While, according to this perspective, the IMF would play the role of a trustee and possibly that of a crisis manager, it would have a limited role as a lender of last resort. There is a shortage of international liquidity available to specific countries that become unable to credibly pledge returns to investors; there is little shortage of international liquidity overall.
- Finally, policies that treat the symptoms rather than the disorders may be misguided. For instance, foreign investors may not be reassured by a lengthening of the maturity of the debt or by its denomination in local currency.

More generally I hope that research building on the dual-agency and common-agency perspectives will provide guidance to identify the set of policies and institutions that will allow Emerging Markets economies to better benefit from their capital account liberalization.

References

Aghion, P., and J. Tirole (1997) "Formal and Real Authority in Organizations," *Journal of Political Economy*, 105: 1–29.

Aghion, P., P. Bacchetta and A. Banerjee (1999) "Financial Liberalization and Volatility in Emerging Market Economies," in: P.R. Agénor, M. Miller, D. Vines and A. Weber (eds), *The Asian Financial Crises: Causes, Contagion and Consequences*, Cambridge: Cambridge University Press, pp167–90.

——— (2001) "Currency Crises and Monetary Policy in an Economy with Credit Constraints," *European Economic Review*, 45: 1121–50.

Allen, F., and D. Gale (1998) "Optimal Financial Crises," *Journal of Finance*, 53: 1245–83.

——— (2000a) "Optimal Currency Crises," University of Pennsylvania and NYU.

——— (2000b) *Comparing Financial Markets*, MIT Press.

America's Council on Foreign Relations (1999) *Safeguarding Property in a Global Financial System*, Institute for International Economics.

Bacchetta, P. (2000) "Monetary Policy with Foreign Currency Debt," University of Lausanne, mimeo.

Bagehot, W. (1873) *Lombard Street: A Description of the Money Market*, London: H.S. King.

Bagwell, K., and R. Staiger (2000) "GATT-Think," mimeo, Columbia University, and University of Wisconsin.

Bartolini, L., and A. Drazen (1997) "Capital-Account Liberalization as a Signal," *American Economic Review*, 87(1): 138–54.

Bernard, H., and J. Bisignano (2000) "Information, Liquidity and Risk in the International Interbank Market: Implicit Guarantees and Private Credit Market Failure," BIS Working Paper, n°86.

Bernheim, D., and M. Whinston (1986a) "Menu Auctions, Resource Allocation, and Economic Influence," *Quarterly Journal of Economics*, 101: 1–33.

—— (1986b) "Common Agency," *Econometrica*, 54: 923–42.

Bhagwati, J. (1998) "The Capital Myth: The Difference Between Trade in Widgets and Trade in Dollars," *Foreign Affairs*, 77: 7–12.

Bizer, D., and P. De Marzo (1992) "Sequential Banking," *Journal of Political Economy*, 100: 41–61.

Bordo, M., M. Eichengreen, D. Klingebiel and M. Soledad Martinez-Peria (2001) "Is the Crisis Problem Growing More Severe?," *Economic Policy*, 32: 51–75.

Brealey, R. (1999) "The Asian Crisis: Lessons for Crisis Management and Prevention," Bank of England and London Business School, mimeo.

Bryant, J. (1980) "A Model of Reserves, Bank Runs, and Deposit Insurance, *Journal of Banking and Finance*, 43: 749–61.

Bulow, J., and K. Rogoff (1988) "Multilateral Negotiations for Rescheduling Developing Country Debt: A Bargaining Theoretic Framework," IMF Staff Papers 35, reprinted in *Analytical Issues in Debt*, Frenkel, J., Dooley, M., and P. Wickham (eds), IMF, Washington DC, 1989.

—— (1989) "A Constant Recontracting Model of Sovereign Debt," *Journal of Political Economy*, 97: 155–78.

Burnside, C., M. Eichenbaum and S. Rebelo (1999) "Prospective Deficits and the Asian Currency Crisis," mimeo.

—— (2000) "On the Fundamentals of Self-Fulfilling Speculative Attacks," University of Rochester, Center for Economic Research WP468.

—— (2001) "Hedging and Financial Fragility in Fixed Exchange Rates Regimes," *European Economic Review*, 45: 1151–94.

Caballero, R. (2000) "Macroeconomic Volatility in Latin America: A View and Three Case Studies," mimeo, MIT.

Caballero, R., and A. Krishnamurthy (1999) 'Emerging Markets Crises: An Asset Markets Perspectives," mimeo, Department of Economics, MIT.

—— (2001a) "Dollarization of Liabilities: Underinsurance and Domestic Financial Development," mimeo, MIT and Northwestern.

—— (2001b) "International Liquidity Illusion: On the Risks of Sterilization," mimeo, MIT and Northwestern.

Calomiris, C.W. (1999) "Moral Hazard is Avoidable," in W. Hunter, G. Kaufman and T. Krueger (eds), *The Asian Financial Crisis:*

Origins, Implications, and Solutions, Kluwer Academic Publishers.

Calomiris, C., and C. Kahn (1991) "The Role of Demandable Debt in Structuring Optimal Banking Arrangements," *American Economic Review*, 81(3): 497–513.

Calomiris, C., and A. Meltzer (1999) "Reforming the IMF," mimeo, Columbia Business School and Carnegie Mellon University.

Calvo, G. (1998) "Balance of Payments Crises in Emerging Markets," mimeo, University of Maryland.

——— (2000) "Capital Markets and the Exchange Rate," University of Maryland and Universidad Di Tella.

——— (2000) "The Case for Hard Pegs in the Brave New World of Global Finance," mimeo, Universities of Maryland and Di Tella.

Caprio, G., and P. Honohan (1999) "Restoring Banking Stability: Beyond Supervised Capital Requirements," *Journal of Economic Perspectives*, 13(4): 43–64.

Chang, R. (1999) "Origins of the Asian Crises: Discussion," in W. Hunter, G. Kaufman and T. Krueger, (eds), *The Asian Financial Crisis: Origins, Implications, and Solutions*, Kluwer Academic Publishers.

Chang, R., and G. Majnoni (2000) "International Contagion: Implications for Policy," paper presented at the World Bank/Asian Development Bank/IMF conference on "International Financial Contagion: How it Spreads, How it Can Be Stopped", Washington, DC, February 3–4.

Chang, R., and A. Velasco (1999) "Liquidity Crises in Emerging Markets: Theory and Policy," in *NBER MacroAnnual*, Bernanke, B. and J. Rotemberg (eds). Cambridge: MIT Press.

Chari, V.V., and P. Kehoe (2001) "Hot Money," Federal Reserve Bank of Minneapolis Research Department Staff Report 228.

Christoffersen, P., and V. Errunza (2000) "Towards a Global Financial Architecture: Capital Mobility and Risk Management Issues," *Emerging Markets Review*, 1: 3–20.

Claessens, S., and I. Diwan (1990) "Investment Incentives: New Money, Debt Relief, and the Critical Role of Conditionality in the Debt Crisis," *World Bank Economic Review*, 4: 21–42.

Claessens, S., S. Djankov and L. Lang (2000) "The Separation of Ownership and Control in East Asian Corporation," *Journal of Financial Economics*, 58 (1–2): 81–112.

Coeuré, B., and J. Pisani-Ferry (2001) "Events, Ideas and Actions: An Intellectual and Institutional Retrospective on the Reform of the

International Financial Architecture," mimeo, Conseil d'Analyse Economique, Paris.

Cole, H., and T. Kehoe (1998) "A Self-Fulfilling Debt Crisis," Federal Reserve of Minneapolis Staff Report 211, July.

Cooper, R. (1984) "A Monetary System for the Future," *Foreign Affairs*, 63: 166–184.

Corsetti, G. (1999) "Interpreting the Asian Financial Crisis: Open Issues in Theory and Policy," *Asian Development Review*, 16.

Corsetti, G., M. Pericolli and M. Sbracia (2000) "A Perspective on Empirical Studies of Contagion and Interdependence," mimeo, Bank of Italy.

Corsetti, G., P. Pesenti and N. Roubini (1999) "What Caused the Asian Currency and Financial Crisis? Part I: A Macroeconomic Overview," mimeo.

De Bijl, P. (1994) "Delegation of Responsibility in Organizations," CentER DP 9469, Tilburg University.

De Bonis, R., A. Giustiniani and G. Gomel (1999) "Crises and Bail-Outs of Banks and Countries: Linkages, Analogies and Differences," *The World Economy*, D. Greenway and J. Whalley (eds), Oxford: Blackwell.

De Gregorio, J., B. Eichengreen, T. Ito and C. Wyplosz (1999) *An Independent and Accountable IMF*, CEPR and ICMB.

De Gregorio, J., and R.O. Valdes (2000) "Crisis Transmission: Evidence from the Debt, Tequila and Asian Flu Crises," paper presented at the World Bank/Asian Development Bank/IMF conference on "International Financial Contagion: How it Spreads, How it Can Be Stopped", Washington, DC, February 3–4.

Detragiache, E., and A. Spilimbergo (2001) "Short-Term Debt and Crises," mimeo, IMF.

Dewatripont, M. and J. Tirole (1994a) *The Prudential Regulation of Banks*, MIT Press.

——— (1994b) "A Theory of Debt and Equity: Diversity of Securities and Manager-Shareholder Congruence," *Quarterly Journal of Economics*, 109 (4): 1027–54.

——— (1996) "Biased Principal as a Discipline Device," *Japan and the World Economy*, 8: 195–206.

——— (1999) "Advocates," *Journal of Political Economy*, 107 (1): 1–39.

Dewatripont, M., I. Jewitt and J. Tirole (1999a) "The Economics of Career Concerns, Part I: Comparing Information Structures," *Review of Economic Studies*, 66(1): 183–98.

────── (1999b) "The Economics of Career Concerns, Part II: Application to Missions and Accountability of Government Agencies," *Review of Economic Studies*, 66(1): 199–217.

Diamond, D., and P. Dybvig (1983) "Bank Runs, Deposit Insurance, and Liquidity," *Journal of Political Economy*, 91: 401–19.

Diamond D., and R. Rajan (2001) "Liquidity Shortages and Banking Crises," mimeo, University of Chicago.

Diaz-Alejandro, C. F. (1985) "Good-bye Financial Repression, Hello Financial Crash." *Journal of Development Economics* 19. Reprinted in A. Velasco (ed), *Trade, Development and the World Economy, Selected Essays of Carlos Diaz-Alejandro*. Oxford, UK: Blackwell, 1988.

Dillinger, W., and S. Webb (1999) "Fiscal Management in Federal Democracies: Argentina and Brazil," Working Paper, World Bank.

Dixit, A. (1996) *The Making of Economic Policy*, MIT Press.

────── (2000) "IMF Programs as Incentive Mechanisms," mimeo, Princeton University.

Dornbusch, R. (1998) "After Asia: New Directions for the International Financial System," Massachusetts Institute of Technology, unpublished manuscript.

Dornbusch, R., Y.C. Park and S. Claessens (2000) "Contagion: How It Spreads and How It Can Be Stopped," paper presented at the World Bank/Asian Development Bank/IMF conference on "International Financial Contagion: How it Spreads, How it Can Be Stopped", Washington, DC, February 3–4.

Eaton, J., and M. Gersovitz (1981) "Debt with Potential Repudiations," *Review of Economic Studies*, 48: 289–309.

Economist, The (1999) "Survey of Global Finance: Time for a Redesign?"

Eichengreen, B. (1999a) *Toward a New International Financial Architecture: A Practical PostAsia Agenda*, Institute for International Economics, Washington D.C.

────── (1999b) "Bailing in the Private Sector," in W. Hunter, G. Kaufman and T. Krueger (eds), *The Asian Financial Crisis: Origins, Implications, and Solutions*, Kluwer Academic Publishers.

────── (2000) "Realistic and Romantic Reforms of the International Financial System," *CES Forum*, Center for Economic Studies, Munich, pp3–8.

Eichengreen, B., and R. Portes (1997) "Managing Financial Crises in Emerging Markets," paper prepared for the Federal Reserve Bank of Kansas City's annual economics conference, Jackson Hole, August 28–30.

Eichengreen, B., and C. Rühl (2000) "The Bail-In Problem: Systematic Goals, Ad Hoc Means," mimeo, UC Berkeley and World Bank.

Feldstein, M. (1998a) "Refocusing the IMF," *Foreign Affairs*, 77: 20–33.

―――― (1998b) "What the IMF Should Do," *Wall Street Journal*, October 6.

Fischer, S. (1998a) "The Asian Crisis: A View from the IMF," paper presented at the Midwinter Conference of the Bankers' Association for Foreign Trade, Washington, DC, January 22.

―――― (1998b) "Economic Crises and the Financial Sector," paper presented at FDIC Conference on Deposit insurance, Washington, DC, September 10.

―――― (1999a) "Reforming the International Financial System," mimeo, IMF.

―――― (1999b) "On the Need for an International Lender of Last Resort," *Journal of Economic Perspectives*, 13: 85–104.

Foreman-Peck, J. (1994) *History of the World Economy : International Economic Relations Since 1850*, 2nd edition, Harvester Wheatsheaf.

French, K., and J. Poterba (1991) "Investor Diversification and International Equity Markets," *American Economic Review*, 81: 222–6.

Freixas, X., and J.C. Rochet (1997) *Microeconomics of Banking*, MIT Press.

Froot, K., D. Scharfstein and J. Stein (1993) "Risk Management: Coordinating Corporate Investment and Financing Policies," *Journal of Finance*, 48: 1629–58.

Frydl, E. (1999) "The Length and Cost of Banking Crises," IMF WP 99/30, Washington DC.

Garber, P. (1998) "Derivatives in International Capital Flow," NBER WP 6623.

Giannini, C. (1999) "Enemy of None but the Common Friend of All? An International Perspective on the Lender-of-Last-Resort Function," *Princeton Essays in International Finance*, n°214.

―――― (2000) "Pitfalls in International Lending," forthcoming in C. Goodhart and G. Illing (eds), *Financial Crises, Contagion and the Lender of Last Resort: A Book of Readings*, Oxford University Press.

Goldfajn, I., and T. Baig (2000) "The Russian Default and the Contagion to Brazil," paper presented at the World Bank/Asian Development Bank/IMF conference on "International Financial Contagion: How it Spreads, How it Can Be Stopped", Washington, DC, February 3–4.

Goldfajn, I., and R. Valdes (1998) "Are Currency Crises Predictable," *European Economic Review*, 42: 873–85.

Goldstein, M. (2001) "IMF Structural Conditionality: How Much is Too Much?" Institute for International Economics Working Paper, April.

Gourinchas, P.O., R. Valdes and O. Landerretche (1999) "Lending Booms: Some Stylized Facts," mimeo, Princeton University, Central Bank of Chile and MIT.

Grossman, G., and E. Helpman (1994) "Protection for Sale," *American Economic Review*, 84: 833–50.

Group of 10 (G-10) (1996) *Resolving Sovereign Liquidity Crises*, Washington DC, G-10.

Group of 22 (G-22) (1998) *Three Reports on International Financial Architecture Reform*.

Haldane, A. (1999) "Private Sector Involvement in Financial Crises: Analytics and Public Policy Approaches," *Financial Stability Review*, Bank of England.

Hansmann, H. (1996) *The Ownership of Enterprise*, Belknap Harvard.

Harberger, A. (1985) "Lessons for Debtor Country Managers and Policy Makers," in G. Smith and J. Cuddington (eds), *International Debt and the Developing Countries*, World Bank.

Hirschman, A. (1970) *Exit, Voice, and Loyalty : Responses to Decline in Firms, Organizations, and States*, Harvard University Press.

Holmström B. (1982) "Moral Hazard in Teams," *Bell Journal of Economics*, 13: 324–40.

Holmström B., and J. Tirole (1996) "Modelling Aggregate Liquidity,"*American Economic Review, Papers and Proceedings*, 86:187–91.

———— (1998) "Private and Public Supply of Liquidity," *Journal of Political Economy*, 106(1): 1–40.

———— (2000) "Liquidity and Risk Management," (JMCB lecture) *Journal of Money, Credit and Banking*, 32 (3): 295–319.

———— (2001a) "LAPM: A Liquidity-Based Asset Pricing Model," *Journal of Finance*, 56: 1837–1867.

—— (2001b) *Inside and Outside Liquidity*, Wicksell Lectures, forthcoming.

—— (2002) "Domestic and International Supply of Liquidity", *American Economic Review Papers and Proceedings*.

Hunter, W., G. Kaufman and T. Krueger (eds) (1999) *The Asian Financial Crisis: Origins, Implications and Solutions*, Boston: Kluwer Academic Press.

International Monetary Fund (1996) *Macroeconomic Consequences and Causes of Bank Unsoundness*, Washington DC.

International Monetary Fund (1999) "The IMF Policy on Lending into Arrears to Private Creditors", mimeo.

Jacquet, P., J. Pisani-Ferry and D. Strauss-Kahn (2000) "Trade Rules and Global Governance: A Long-Term Agenda," mimeo, Conseil d'Analyse Economique, Paris.

Jeanne, O. (1998) "The International Liquidity Mismatch and the New Architecture," mimeo, IMF.

—— (1999a) "Foreign Currency Debt and the Global Financial Architecture," *European Economic Review Papers and Proceedings*, 44: 719–27.

—— (1999b) "Foreign Currency Debt and Signaling," mimeo, IMF.

—— (2000) "Debt Maturity and the Global Financial Architecture," CEPR DP2520.

Jeanne, O., and C. Wyplosz (2001) "The International Lender of Last Resort: How Large is Large Enough?" WP 01/76 & CEPR DP 2842, forthcoming in M. Dooley, and J. Frankel (eds), *Managing Currency Crises in Emerging Markets*, NBER.

Jeanne, O., and J. Zettelmeyer (2000) "International Bailouts, Financial Transparency, and Moral Hazard," mimeo, IMF.

—— (2001) "International Bailouts, Moral Hazard, and Conditionality," prepared for the Economic Policy Panel Meeting, Stockholm, 33: 409–32.

Jensen, M. (1986) "Agency Costs of Free Cash Flow, Corporate Finance and Takeovers," *American Economic Review*, 76: 323–29.

Jensen, M. and W.R. Meckling (1976) "Theory of the Firm, Managerial Behaviour, Agency Costs and Ownership Structure," *Journal of Financial Economics*, 3: 305–60.

Johnson, O. (1997) "Policy Reform as Collective Action," IMF Working Paper n°163.

Kahn, M., and S. Sharma (2001) "IMF Conditionality and Country Ownership of Programs," mimeo, IMF.

Kaminsky, G., and C. Reinhart (1999) "The Twin Crises: The Causes of Banking and Balance-of-Payments Problems," *American Economic Review*, 89(3): 473–500.

Kaminsky, G., R. Lyons and S. Schmukler (2000) "Economic Fragility, Liquidity, and Risk: The Behavior of Mutual Funds during Crisis," paper presented at the World Bank/Asian Development Bank/IMF conference on "International Financial Contagion: How it Spreads, How it Can Be Stopped", Washington, DC, February 3–4.

Kaplan, S., and P. Strömberg (1999) "Financial Contracting Theory Meets the Real World: An Empirical Analysis of Venture Capital Contracts," mimeo.

—— (2000) "How Do Venture Capitalists Choose Investments?," mimeo, Graduate School of Business, University of Chicago.

Kaufman, G., and T. Krueger (eds), *The Asian Financial Crisis*.

Kaufman, H. (1998) "Preventing the Next Global Financial Crisis," *Washington Post*, January 28, A17.

Kenen, P. (2001) "The International Financial Architecture. What's New? What's Missing?," Forthcoming, Institute for International Analysis, Washington.

Kiyotaki, N., and J. Moore (2000) "Inside Money and Liquidity," mimeo, London School of Economics.

Kraay, A., N. Loayza, L. Serven and J. Ventura (2000) "Country Portfolios," mimeo, World Bank and MIT.

Krugman, P. (1979) "A Model of Balance of Payments Crises," *Journal of Money, Credit and Banking*, 11: 311–25.

—— (1999a) "Balance Sheets, The Transfer Problem, and Financial Crises," in *International Finance and Financial Crises, Essays in Honor of Robert Flood Jr*, Isard, P. Razin, A. and A. Rose (eds), Kluwer Academic Publishers and IMF, 31–44.

—— (1999b) "Fire-Sale FDI," mimeo, MIT.

Kumar, M., P. Masson and M. Miller (2000) "Global Financial Crises: Institutions and Incentives," IMF WP/00/105.

Lewis, K. (1999) "Trying to Explain Home Bias in Equities and Consumption," *Journal of Economic Literature*, 37: 571–608.

Litan, R. (1999) "Does the IMF Have a Future? What Should It Be?," in W. Hunter, G. Kaufman and T. Krueger (eds), *The Asian Financial Crises: Origins, Implications, and Solutions*, Kluwer Academic Publishers.

Maggi, G., and A. Rodriguez-Clare (1998) "The Value of Trade Agreements in the Presence of Political Pressures," *Journal of Political Economy*, 106: 574–601.

Martimort, D. (1992) "Multiprincipaux avec Antisélection", *Annales d'Economie et de Statistique*, 28: 1–38.

——— (1999) "Renegotiation Design with Multiple Regulators," *Journal of Economic Theory*, 88: 261–93.

Maskin, E. and J. Tirole (2001) "The Politician and the Judge: Accountability in Government," mimeo.

Masson, P. (1999a) "Contagion in Macroeconomic Models with Multiple Equilibria," *Journal of International Money and Finance*, 18(4): 587–602.

——— (1999b) "Contagion: Monsoonal Effects, Spillovers and Jumps Between Multiple Equilibria," *The Asian Financial Crises: Causes, Contagion and Consequences*, P. R. Agénor, M. Miller, D. Vines and A. Weber (eds), Cambridge: Cambridge University Press.

McKinnon, R., and H. Pill (1990) "Credible Liberalization and International Capital Flows: The 'Overborrowing Syndrom'," in *Financial Deregulation and Integration in East Asia*, T. Ito and A. Krueger (eds), Chicago: University of Chicago Press.

Meltzer Report (2000) *International Financial Institutions Reform: Report of the International Financial Institution Advisory Commission*: http:// www.ids.ac.uk/eldis/ifiac.html.

Monfort, B., and C. Mulder (2000) "Using Credit Ratings for Capital Requirements on Lending to Emerging Markets Economies: Possible Impact of a New Basel Accord," IMF WP0069.

Morris, S., and H. Shin (1998) "Unique Equilibrium in a Model of Self-Fulfilling Currency Attacks," *American Economic Review*, 88: 587–97.

Mussa, M. (1999) "Reforming the International Financial Architecture: Limiting Moral Hazard and Containing Real Hazard," mimeo, IMF.

Mussa, M., and M. Savastano (1999) "The IMF Approach to Economic Stabilization," IMF Research Department WP99/104.

Mussa, M., A. Swoboda, J. Zettelmeyer and O. Jeanne (1999) "Moderating Fluctuations in Capital Flows to Emerging Market Economies," Forthcoming as Chapter 4 of *Reforming the International Monetary and Financial System*, P. Kenen and A. Swoboda (eds), International Monetary Fund.

Myers, S. and N. Majluf (1984) "Corporate Financing and Investment Decisions When Firms Have Information that Investors Do Not Have," *Journal of Financial Economics*, 13: 187–221.

Obstfeld, M. (1998) "The Global Capital Market : Benefactor or Menace ?" *Journal of Economic Perspectives*, 12 : 81-101.

Obstfeld, M., and K. Rogoff (1998) *Foundations of International Macroeconomics*, 3rd edition, MIT Press.

Olsen, T., and G. Torsvik (1993) "The Ratchet Effect in Common Agency: Implications for Regulation and Privatization," *Journal of Law, Economics, and Organization*, 9(1): 136–58.

——— (1995) "Intertemporal Common Agency and Organizational Design: How Much Decentralization?," *European Economic Review*, 39(7): 1405–28.

Pauly, M.V. (1974) "Overinsurance and Public Provision of Insurance: The Roles of Moral Hazard and Adverse Selection," *Quarterly Journal of Economics*; 88(1): 44–62.

Portes, R. (1999) "An Analysis of Financial Crisis: Lessons for the International Financial System," in W. Hunter, G. Kaufman and T. Krueger (eds), *The Asian Financial Crisis: Origins, Implications, and Solutions*, Kluwer Academic Publishers.

——— (2000) "Sovereign Debt Restructuring: The Role of Institutions for Collective Action," mimeo, LBS and CEPR.

Radelet, S., and J. Sachs (1998) "The East Asian Crisis: Diagnosis, Remedies, Prospects," *Brookings Papers on Economic Activity*, 1: 1–90.

Rey, P., and J. Stiglitz (1994) "Short-Term Contracts as a Monitoring Device," NBER WP#4514.

Rochet, J.C., and X. Vives (2000) "Systemic Risk and the Lender of Last Resort," mimeo.

Rodrik, D. (1996) "Why is There Multilateral Lending?", *Annual World Bank Conference on Development Economics 1995*, pp167–205.

Rogoff, K. (1999) "International Institutions for Reducing Global Financial Instability," *Journal of Economic Perspectives*, 13: 21–42.

Rojas-Suarez, L., and S. Weisbrod (1996) "Banking Crises in Latin America: Experiences and Issues," in Hausmann, R. and L. Rojas-Suarez (eds), *Banking Crises in Latin America*, Washington D.C.: IADB.

Ross, S. (1977) "The Determination of Financial Structure: The Incentive Signalling Approach," *Bell Journal of Economics*, 8: 23–40.

Roubini, N. (2000) "Bail-In, Burden Sharing, Private Sector Involvement (PSI) in Crisis Resolution and Constructive Engagement of the Private Sector," mimeo, NYU.

Sachs, J. (1990) "Conditionality, Debt Relief, and the Developing Countries' Debt Crisis," in J. Sachs, (ed), *Developing Country Debt and Economic Performance: The International Financial System*, vol. 1, University of Chicago Press.

――― (1995) "Do We Need an International Lender of Last Resort?" Princeton University, Frank Graham Memorial Lecture.

――― (1997) "IMF is a Power unto Itself," mimeo.

Sachs, J., and S. Radelet (1998) "The East Asian Financial Crisis: Diagnosis, Remedies, Prospects." *Brookings Papers on Economic Activity*, 1(l):74.

Sachs, J., and A. Warner (1995) "Economic Reform and the Process of Global Integration," *Brookings Papers on Economic Activity*, 1: 1–118.

Sachs, J., and W. T. Woo (2000) "A Reform Agenda for a Resilient Asia," chapter 1 in W.T. Woo, J. Sachs, *The Asian Financial Crisis: Lessons for a Resilient Asia*, MIT Press.

Schwarcz, S. (2000) "Sovereign Debt Restructuring: A Bankruptcy Reorganization Approach," *Cornell Law Review*, 85.

Schwartz, A.J. (1999) "Assessing IMF's Crisis Prevention and Management Record," in W. Hunter, G. Kaufman and T. Krueger (eds), *The Asian Financial Crisis: Origins, Implications, and Solutions*, Kluwer Academic Publishers.

Segal, I. (1999) "Contracting with Externalities," *Quarterly Journal of Economics*, 114 (2): 337–88.

Soros, G. (1998) *The Crisis of Global Capitalism*, New York: Public Affairs Press.

Spence, M. (1974) *Market Signaling*, Cambridge, Mass.: Harvard University Press.

Stallings, B. (1979) "Peru and the US Banks: Privatization of Financial Relations," in R. Fagen, (ed), *Capitalism and the State in US-Latin American Relations*, Stanford: Stanford University Press.

Stiglitz, J. (1998) "The Role of International Financial Institutions in the Current Global Economy," address to the Chicago Council on Foreign Relations, Chicago, February 27.

Stole, L. (1991) "Mechanism Design under Common Agency," chapter 1 in PhD thesis, MIT, Department of Economics.

Summers, L. (1999) "Reflections on Managing Global Integration," *Journal of Economic Perspectives*, 13: 3–18.

—— (2000) "International Financial Crises: Causes, Prevention and Cures," (Richard Ely Lecture) *American Economic Review Papers and Proceedings*, 90: 1–16.

Tirole, J. (2001) "Corporate Governance," *Econometrica*, 69 (1): 1–35.

Tornell, A, and A. Velasco (2000) "Fixed vs Flexible Exchange Rates: Which Provides More Fiscal Discipline?," *Journal of Monetary Economics*, 45: 399–436.

Van Rijckeghem, C., and B. Weder (2000) "Financial Contagion: Spillovers through Banking Centers," paper presented at the World Bank/Asian Development Bank/IMF conference on "International Financial Contagion: How it Spreads, How it Can Be Stopped", Washington, DC, February 3–4.

Wilson, J. Q. (1989) *Bureaucracy: What Government Agencies Do and Why They Do It*, New York: Basic Books.

Williamson, J. (1996) *The Crawling Band as an Exchange Rate Regime: Lessons from Chile, Columbia and Israel*, Institute for International Economics, Washington DC.

—— (2000) "Exchange Rate Regimes for Emerging Markets: Reviving the Intermediate Option," Policy Analyses in International Economics 60, Institute for International Economics, Washington DC.

Woo, W.T., Sachs, J. and K. Schwab (2000) *The Asian Financial Crisis: Lessons for a Resilient Asia*, MIT Press.

World Bank (1997) *Private Capital Flows to Developing Countries*, Oxford University Press.

World Bank (1998) *East Asia: The Road to Recovery*, Washington DC.

World Economic Outlook (1998) *Financial Turbulence and The World Economy*, International Monetary Fund, October.

Index